Arabic
Phrases
FOR
DUMMIES®

by Amine Bouchentouf

Wiley Publishing, Inc.

Arabic Phrases For Dummies®

Published by
Wiley Publishing, Inc.
111 River St.
Hoboken, NJ 07030-5774
www.wiley.com

Copyright © 2009 by Wiley Publishing, Inc., Indianapolis, Indiana

Published by Wiley Publishing, Inc., Indianapolis, Indiana

Published simultaneously in Canada

For general information on our other products and services, please contact our Customer Care Department within the U.S. at 800-762-2974, outside the U.S. at 317-572-3993, or fax 317-572-4002.

For technical support, please visit www.wiley.com/techsupport.

Wiley also publishes its books in a variety of electronic formats. Some content that appears in print may not be available in electronic books.

Library of Congress Control Number: 2008923127

ISBN: 978-0-470-22523-3

Manufactured in the United States of America

10 9 8 7 6 5 4 3 2

WILEY

About the Author

Amine Bouchentouf is a native English, Arabic, and French speaker born and raised in Casablanca, Morocco. Amine has been teaching Arabic and lecturing about relations between America and the Arab world in his spare time for over four years and has offered classes and seminars for students at Middlebury College, the Council on Foreign Relations, and various schools across the United States. He runs and maintains the Web site www.al-baab.com (which means "gateway" in Arabic).

Amine graduated from Middlebury College and has always been interested in promoting better relations between the West and the Middle East through dialogue and mutual understanding. Amine published his first book, *Arabic: A Complete Course* (Random House), soon after graduating college in order to help Americans understand Arabic language and culture. He has written *Arabic For Dummies* and *Arabic Phrases For Dummies* in an attempt to reach an even wider audience with the aim of fostering better relations through education.

He holds a degree in Economics from Middlebury and has extensive experience in the arena of international investing. He is a registered investment advisor and a member of the National Association of Securities Dealers. He is also the author of *Commodities For Dummies*.

Amine lives in New York City with his wife, Tracy. He is an avid traveler and has visited over 15 countries across the Middle East, Europe, and North and South America. Aside from his interest in languages, business, and travel, Amine enjoys biking, rollerblading, playing guitar, chess, and golf.

Publisher's Acknowledgments

We're proud of this book; please send us your comments through our Dummies online registration form located at www.dummies.com/register/.

Some of the people who helped bring this book to market include the following:

Acquisitions, Editorial, and Media Development

Compiler:
Laura Peterson Nussbaum

Project Editor: Joan Friedman

Acquisitions Editor:
Lindsay Sandman Lefevere

Assistant Editor:
Erin Calligan Mooney

Editorial Program Coordinator: Joe Niesen

Senior Editorial Manager:
Jennifer Ehrlich

Editorial Supervisor:
Carmen Krikorian

Editorial Assistant:
Jennette ElNaggar

Cartoons: Rich Tennant,
www.the5thwave.com

Composition

Project Coordinator:
Patrick Redmond

Layout and Graphics:
Reuben W. Davis,
Stephanie D. Jumper,
Christine Williams

Proofreaders:
Caitie Copple,
Melissa Cossell,
Shannon Ramsey

Indexer: Claudia Bourbeau

Publishing and Editorial for Consumer Dummies

> **Diane Graves Steele,** Vice President and Publisher, Consumer Dummies

> **Kristin Ferguson-Wagstaffe,** Product Development Director, Consumer Dummies

> **Ensley Eikenburg,** Associate Publisher, Travel

> **Kelly Regan,** Editorial Director, Travel

Publishing for Technology Dummies

> **Andy Cummings,** Vice President and Publisher, Dummies Technology/General User

Composition Services

> **Gerry Fahey,** Vice President of Production Services

> **Debbie Stailey,** Director of Composition Services

Table of Contents

● ●

Introduction *1*

   About This Book 1
   Conventions Used in This Book 2
   Foolish Assumptions 3
   Icons Used in This Book 3
   Where to Go from Here 4

Chapter 1: I Say It How? Speaking Arabic **5**

   Taking Stock of What's Familiar 5
   Discovering the Arabic Alphabet 7
      All about vowels 7
      All about consonants 10
   Tackling Tough Letters and Words 15
   Addressing Arabic Transcription 15

Chapter 2: Grammar on a Diet: Just the Basics **17**

   Introducing Nouns, Adjectives, and Articles 17
      Getting a grip on nouns 18
      Identifying adjectives 18
      Discovering definite and indefinite articles
         (and the sun and moon) 19
      Understanding the interaction between
         nouns and adjectives 21
   Creating Simple, Verb-Free Sentences 23
      To be or not to be: Sentences without verbs 23
      Building sentences with
         common prepositions 25
      Using demonstratives and forming sentences ... 26
      Forming "to be" sentences using
         personal pronouns 28
      Creating negative "to be" sentences 30
      "To be" in the past tense 32
   Working with Verbs 33
      Digging up the past tense 33
      Examining the present tense 36
      Peeking into the future tense 39

**Chapter 3: Numerical Gumbo:
Counting of All Kinds** **41**

   Talking Numbers 41
   Discovering Ordinal Numbers 43

Telling Time in Arabic......................................45
    Specifying the time of day 46
    Specifying minutes 47
Referring to Days and Months 49
Money, Money, Money......................................52
    Opening a bank account 52
    Using the ATM 54
    Exchanging currency...55

**Chapter 4: Making New Friends and
Enjoying Small Talk 57**

Greetings!...57
    You say hello 58
    . . . I say goodbye 58
    How are you doing?..59
    I'm doing well! 59
Making Introductions...60
    Asking "What's your name?" 60
    Responding with "My name is . . ." 60
Talking about Countries and Nationalities............61
    Asking "Where are you from?"..............................61
    Answering "I am from . . ." 62
Asking Questions...63
Talking about Yourself and Your Family.................65
Talking about Work..67
Shooting the Breeze: Talking about the Weather....69

**Chapter 5: Enjoying a Drink or a Snack
(or a Meal!) 73**

All about Meals 73
    Breakfast 74
    Lunch...76
    Dinner..81
Enjoying a Meal at Home 82
Dining Out..83
    Perusing the menu..83
    Placing your order..85
    Finishing your meal and paying the bill.............87

Chapter 6: Shop 'til You Drop! 89

Going to the Store..89
    Browsing the merchandise....................................90
    Getting around the store 91
Asking for a Particular Item 92

Comparing Merchandise 95
    Comparing two or more items 95
    Picking out the best item 98
Shopping for Clothes 100

Chapter 7: Making Leisure a Top Priority 103

Visiting Museums 103
Going to the Movies 106
Touring Religious Sites 109
    A few rules to keep in mind 109
    The Hajj 110
Sporting an Athletic Side 111
Going to the Beach 115
Playing Musical Instruments 115
Popular Hobbies 116

Chapter 8: When You Gotta Work 119

Landing a Job 119
Managing the Office Environment 122
    Interacting with your colleagues 124
    Giving orders 129
    Supplying your office 131
Picking Up the Phone 132
    Dialing up the basics 132
    Beginning a phone conversation 132
    Asking to speak to someone 133
    Making business appointments 133
    Dealing with voice mail 135

Chapter 9: I Get Around: Transportation 137

Traveling by Plane 137
    Making reservations 137
    Getting some legwork out of
       the verb "to travel" 140
    Registering at the airport 141
    Boarding the plane 143
    A brief departure on the verb "to arrive" 144
    Going through immigration and customs 145
Getting Around on Land 147
    Hailing a taxi 148
    Taking a bus 149
    Boarding a train 150
Asking for Directions 151
    Asking "where" questions 151
    Answering "where" questions 151

Asking with courtesy.................................. 153
Could you repeat that?........................... 153
Using command forms 155

Chapter 10: Laying Down Your Weary Head: Hotel or Home **159**

Choosing the Right Accommodation 160
Making a Reservation.................................. 162
Figuring out the price............................. 163
Indicating the length of your stay..................... 164
Checking In to the Hotel 165
Checking Out of the Hotel 167
Life at Home 168

Chapter 11: Dealing with Emergencies **171**

Shouting Out for Help 171
A little help with the verb "to help" 172
Lending a hand.................................... 175
Getting Medical Help................................ 176
Locating the appropriate doctor 176
Talking about your body 177
Explaining your symptoms....................... 178
Getting treatment 179
Acquiring Legal Help................................ 180

Chapter 12: Ten Favorite Arabic Expressions..... **183**

marHaba bikum! 183
mumtaaz! 183
al-Hamdu li-llah 184
inshaa' allah 184
mabruk! 185
bi 'idni allah 185
bi SaHHa 185
taHiyyaat.. 186
muballagh 186
tabaaraka allah 187

Chapter 13: Ten Great Arabic Proverbs **189**

al-'amthaal noor al-kalaam. 189
'a'mal khayr wa 'ilqahu fii al-baHr. 189
'uTlubuu al-'ilm min al-mahd 'ilaa al-laHd. 190
yad waaHida maa tusaffiq. 190
al-Harbaa' laa Yughaadir shajaratuh hattaa
yakun mu'akkid 'an shajara 'ukhraa. 190

khaTa' ma'roof 'aHsan min Haqiiqa
ghayr ma'roofa. 191
as-sirr mithel al-Hamaama: 'indamaa
yughaadir yadii yaTiir. 191
al-'aql li an-niDHaar wa al-kalb li as-simaa'............. 192
kul yawm min Hayaatuk SafHa min taariikhuk. 192
li faatik bi liila faatik bi Hiila.................................... 192

Index.. 193

The 5th Wave

By Rich Tennant

"I think your Arabic is coming along fine for your trip to Casablanca, with or without the Humphrey Bogart impression."

Introduction

. . . .

*A*rabic, the official language of more than 20 countries, is the mother tongue of more than 300 mil-
lion people. It's spoken throughout the Middle East,
from Morocco to Iraq. Also, because Arabic is the
language of the Koran and Islam, it's understood by
more than 1.2 billion people across the world.

Due to recent geopolitical events, Arabic has cata-
pulted to the top of the list of important world languages. Even in countries where Arabic isn't the
official language, people are scrambling to master this
vital global language.

Arabic Phrases For Dummies is designed to equip you
with phrases necessary to function in many life situations, from shopping to visiting the theater. So buckle
up and enjoy the journey!

About This Book

Arabic Phrases For Dummies is modular in nature;
every chapter is organized in such a way that you
don't have to read the whole book in order to understand the topic that's discussed. Feel free to jump
through chapters and sections to suit your specific
needs. Also, every grammatical and linguistic point is
explained in plain English so that you can incorporate
the concept immediately.

There are basically three different types of Arabic:
Koranic Arabic, local dialects, and Modern Standard
Arabic:

✓ **Koranic Arabic** is the Arabic used to write the
Koran, the holy book for Muslims. This form of
Arabic is very rigid and hasn't changed much
since the Koran was written approximately

1,500 years ago. Koranic Arabic is widely used in religious circles for prayer, discussions of Islamic issues, and serious deliberations. Its usage is limited primarily within a strict religious context. It's the equivalent of Biblical English.

✔ **The regional dialects** are the most informal type of Arabic. They tend to fall into three geographical categories: the North African dialect (Morocco, Algeria, Tunisia, and Libya); the Egyptian dialect (Egypt, parts of Syria, Palestine, and Jordan); and Gulf Arabic (Saudi Arabia, Kuwait, Iraq, Qatar, and the United Arab Emirates). Even though the words are pronounced differently and some of the everyday expressions differ dramatically from region to region, speakers from different regions can understand each other.

✔ **Modern Standard Arabic (MSA)** is the most widely used and understood form of Arabic in the world. While it's not the native language of any speaker of Arabic, it's used in schools, news broadcasts, and other formal settings. It's less rigid than Koranic Arabic but more formal than the local dialects.

This book focuses on MSA, but I include examples from regional dialects as well.

Conventions Used in This Book

Here are a couple key conventions I use throughout the book:

✔ I present Arabic phrases in *transliteration* (Arabic sounds represented with English characters). You can see the Arabic alphabet in Chapter 1.

✔ Throughout the book, each new Arabic word appears in **boldface.** It's followed by its pronunciation and its English translation in parentheses.

Foolish Assumptions

In writing *Arabic Phrases For Dummies,* I made the following assumptions about my readers:

- ✔ You've had little or no exposure to the Arabic language, or else you've been exposed to Arabic but need to brush up on your language skills.

- ✔ You're interested in mastering Arabic for either personal or professional reasons.

- ✔ You want to be able to speak a few words and phrases now so that you can communicate basic information in Arabic.

Icons Used in This Book

To help you get in and get out of this book easily and efficiently, I use icons that identify important pieces of information by category. The following icons appear in this book:

 When you see this icon, read carefully. It points to information that will directly improve your Arabic language skills.

 I use this icon to bring your attention to information that you definitely want to keep in mind when studying and practicing Arabic.

 Even though this isn't a grammar book, it does include important grammar lessons you need to be aware of. This icon is attached to major grammar points that will help you learn and use the Arabic language.

 This icon points out nonverbal methods of communication common in Arabic-speaking countries and among Arabic speakers. I use this icon to fill the gap between language and culture so that you know the cultural contexts in which you can use newly discovered words and phrases.

Where to Go from Here

Go ahead and start anywhere. You don't have to go in a specific order. Just choose a topic that seems appealing, find the corresponding chapter in the table of contents, and start learning Arabic!

But if you've never taken Arabic before, you may want to read Chapters 1 and 2 before tackling the later chapters. They give you some basics, such as how to pronounce the sounds.

Chapter 1

I Say It How?
Speaking Arabic

. . . .

In This Chapter

▶ Discovering English words that come from Arabic

▶ Figuring out the Arabic alphabet

▶ Practicing the sounds

. . . .

MarHaba (*mahr-hah-bah;* welcome) to the wonderful world of Arabic! In this chapter, I ease
you into the language by showing you some familiar
English words that trace their roots to Arabic. You
discover the Arabic alphabet and its beautiful letters,
and I give you tips on how to pronounce those letters.

Part of exploring a new language is discovering a new
culture and a new way of looking at things, so in this
first chapter of *Arabic Phrases For Dummies,* you begin
your discovery of Arabic and its unique characteristics.

Taking Stock of What's Familiar

If English is your primary language, part of grasping
a new **lougha** (*loo-ghah;* language) is creating con-
nections between the **kalimaat** (*kah-lee-maht;* words)
of the **lougha,** in this case Arabic and English. You
may be surprised to hear that quite a few English
words trace their origins to Arabic. For example, did
you know that "magazine," "candy," and "coffee" are

actually Arabic words? Table 1-1 lists some familiar English words with Arabic origins.

Table 1-1	Arabic Origins of English Words	
English	*Arabic Origin*	*Arabic Meaning*
admiral	amir al-baHr	Ruler of the Sea
alcohol	al-kuHul	a mixture of powdered antimony
alcove	al-qubba	a dome or arch
algebra	al-jabr	to reduce or consolidate
almanac	al-manakh	a calendar
arsenal	daar As-SinaaH	house of manufacture
azure	al-azward	lapis lazuli
candy	qand	cane sugar
coffee	qahwa	coffee
cotton	quTun	cotton
elixir	al-iksiir	philosopher's stone
gazelle	ghazaal	gazelle
hazard	az-zahr	dice
magazine	al-makhzan	a storehouse; a place of storage
mattress	matraH	a place where things are thrown
ream	rizma	a bundle
saffron	za'fran	saffron
Sahara	SaHraa'	desert
satin	zaytuun	Arabic name for a Chinese city
sherbet	sharaba	to drink
sofa	Sofaa	a cushion
sugar	sukkar	sugar
zero	Sifr	zero

As you can see from the table, Arabic has had a major influence on the English language. Some English words such as "admiral" and "arsenal" have an indirect Arabic origin, whereas others, such as "coffee" and "cotton," are exact matches. The influence runs the other way, too, especially when it comes to relatively contemporary terms. For example, the word **tilifizyuun** (*tee-lee-fee-zee-yoon;* television) comes straight from the word "television."

Discovering the Arabic Alphabet

Unlike English and other Romance languages, you write and read Arabic from right to left. Like English, Arabic has both vowels and consonants, but the vowels in Arabic aren't actual letters. Rather, Arabic vowels are symbols that you place on top of or below consonants to create certain sounds. As for consonants, Arabic has 28 different consonants, and each one is represented by a letter. In order to vocalize these letters, you place a vowel above or below the particular consonant. For example, when you put a **fatHa,** a vowel representing the "ah" sound, above the consonant representing the letter "b," you get the sound "bah." When you take the same consonant and use a **kasra,** which represents the "ee" sound, you get the sound "bee."

All about vowels

Arabic has three main vowels. Luckily, they're very simple to pronounce because they're similar to English vowels. However, it's important to realize that Arabic also has vowel derivatives that are as important as the main vowels. These vowel derivatives fall into three categories: *double vowels, long vowels,* and *diphthongs.* In this section, I walk you through all the different vowels, vowel derivatives, and vowel combinations.

Main vowels

The three main Arabic vowels are:

✔ **fatHah:** The first main vowel in Arabic is called a **fatHa** (*feht-hah*). A **fatHa** is the equivalent of the short "a" in "hat" or "cat." Occasionally, a **fatHa** also sounds like the short "e" in "bet" or "set." Much like the other vowels, the way you pronounce a **fatHa** depends on what consonants come before or after it. In Arabic script, the **fatHa** is written as a small horizontal line above a consonant. In English transcription, which I use in this book, it's simply represented by the letter "a," as in the words **kalb** (*kah-leb;* dog) or **walad** (*wah-lahd;* boy).

✔ **damma:** The second main Arabic vowel is the **damma** (*dah-mah*). A **damma** sounds like the "uh" in "foot" or "book." In Arabic script, it's written like a tiny backward "e" above a particular consonant. In English transcription, it's represented by the letter "u," as in **funduq** (*foon-dook;* hotel) or **suHub** (*soo-hoob;* clouds).

✔ **kasra:** The third main vowel in Arabic is the **kasra** (*kahs-rah*), which sounds like the long "e" in "feet" or "treat." The **kasra** is written the same way as a **fatHa** — as a small horizontal line — except that it goes underneath the consonant. In English transcription, it's written as an "i," as in **bint** (*bee-neht;* girl) or **'islaam** (*ees-lahm;* Islam).

Double vowels

One type of vowel derivative is the double vowel, which is known in Arabic as **tanwiin** (*tahn-ween*). The process of **tanwiin** is a fairly simple one: Basically, you take a main vowel and place the same vowel right next to it, thus creating two vowels, or a double vowel. The sound that the double vowel makes depends on the main vowel that's doubled. Here are all possible combinations of double vowels:

✔ **Double fatHa: tanwiin** with **fatHa** creates the "an" sound, as in **'ahlan wa sahlan** (*ahel-an wah sahel-an;* Hi).

✔ **Double damma: tanwiin** with **damma** creates the "oun" sound. For example, **kouratoun** (*koo-rah-toon;* ball) contains a double **damma**.

✔ **Double kasra: tanwiin** with **kasra** makes the "een" sound, as in **SafHatin** (*sahf-hah-teen;* page).

Long vowels

Long vowels are derivatives that elongate the main vowels. Think of the difference between long vowels and short (main) vowels in terms of a musical beat, and you should be able to differentiate between them much more easily. If a main vowel lasts for one beat, then its long vowel equivalent lasts for two beats. Whereas you create double vowels by writing two main vowels next to each other, you create long vowels by adding a letter to one of the main vowels. Each main vowel has a corresponding consonant that elongates it. Here are a few examples to help you get your head around this long-vowel process:

✔ To create a long vowel form of a **fatHa**, you attach an **'alif** to the consonant that the **fatHa** is associated with. In English transcription, the long **fatHa** form is written as "aa," such as in **kitaab** (*kee-taab;* book) or **baab** (*bahb;* door). The "aa" means that you hold the vowel sound for two beats as opposed to one.

✔ The long vowel form of **damma** is obtained by attaching a **waaw** to the consonant with the **damma**. This addition elongates the vowel "uh" into a more pronounced "uu," such as in **nuur** (*noohr;* light) or **ghuul** (*ghoohl;* ghost). Make sure you hold the "uu" vowel for two beats and not one.

✔ To create a long vowel form of a **kasra**, you attach a **yaa'** to the consonant with the **kasra**. Just as the **'alif** elongates the **fatHa** and the **waaw** elongates the **damma**, the **yaa'** elongates the **kasra**. Some examples include the "ii" in words like **kabiir** (*kah-beer;* big) and **Saghiir** (*sah-gheer;* small).

The Arabic characters for the long vowels are shown in Table 1-2.

Table 1-2	Arabic Vowel Characters	
Arabic	*Name of the Character*	*Explanation*
ا	'alif	To create a long vowel form of a fatHa
و	waaw	To create a long vowel form of a damma
ي	yaa'	To create a long vowel form of a kasra

Diphthongs

Diphthongs in Arabic are a special category of vowels because, in essence, they're monosyllabic sounds that begin with one vowel and glide into another vowel. A common example in English is the sound at the end of the word "toy." Fortunately, Arabic has only two diphthong sounds used to distinguish between the **yaa'** and the **waaw** forms of long vowels. When you come across either of these two letters, one of the first questions to ask yourself is: "Is this a long vowel or a diphthong?" There's an easy way to determine which is which: When either the **yaa'** or the **waaw** is a diphthong, you see a **sukun** (*soo-koon*) above the consonant. A **sukun** is similar to the main vowels in that it's a little symbol (a small circle) that you place above the consonant. However, unlike the vowels, you don't vocalize the **sukun** — it's almost like a silent vowel. So when a **waaw** or **yaa'** has a **sukun** over it, you know that the sound is a diphthong. Here are some examples:

- ✔ **waaw** diphthongs: **yawm** (*yah-oom;* day); **nawm** (*nah-oom;* sleep); **Sawt** (*sah-oot;* noise)

- ✔ **yaa'** diphthongs: **bayt** (*bah-yet;* house); **'ayn** (*ah-yen;* eye); **layla** (*lah-ye-lah;* night)

All about consonants

Arabic uses 28 different consonants, and each consonant is represented by a different letter. Because the Arabic alphabet is written in cursive, most of the letters connect with each other. For this reason, every single letter that represents a consonant actually can be written four different ways depending on its position in a word — whether it's in the initial, medial, or final position, or whether it stands alone. In English transcription of the Arabic script, all letters are case-sensitive.

Thankfully, most of the consonants in Arabic have English equivalents. Unfortunately, a few Arabic consonants are quite foreign to nonnative speakers. Table 1-3 shows all 28 Arabic consonants, how they're written in Arabic, how they're transcribed in English, and how they sound.

Table 1-3		Arabic Consonants		
Arabic Character	**Name of the Letter**	**Pronunciation**	***Sounds Like . . .***	***Example***
١	'alif ('a)	*ah-leef*	Sounds like the "a" in "apple"	'ab (*ah-b;* father)
ب	baa' (b)	*bah*	Sounds like the "b" in "boy"	baab (*bahb;* door)
ت	taa' (t)	*tah*	Sounds like the "t" in "table"	tilmiidh (*teel-meez;* student)
ث	thaa' (th)	*thah*	Sounds like the "th" in "think"	thalaatha (*thah-lah-thah;* three)
ج	jiim (j)	*jeem*	Sounds like the "s" in "measure"	jamiil (*jah-meel;* pretty)
ح	Haa' (H)	*hah*	No equivalent in English; imagine the sound you make when you want to blow on your reading glasses to clean them; that soft, raspy noise that comes out is the letter Haa'.	Harr (*hah-r;* hot)
خ	khaa' (kh)	*khah*	Sounds a lot like "Bach" in German or "Baruch" in Hebrew	khuukh (*kh-oo-kh;* peach)
د	daal (d)	*dahl*	Sounds like the "d" in dog	daar (*dah-r;* house)

(continued)

Table 1-3 *(continued)*

Arabic Character	Name of the Letter	Pronun- ciation	Sounds Like ...	Example
ذ	dhaal (dh)	*dhahl*	Sounds like the "th" in those	dhahab (*thah-hab*; gold)
ر	raa' (r)	*rah*	Like the Spanish "r," rolled really fast	rajul (*rah-jool*; man)
ز	zaay (z)	*zay*	Sounds like the "z" in "zebra"	zawja (*zah-oo-ja*; wife)
س	siin (s)	*seen*	Sounds like the "s" in "snake"	samak (*sah-mahk*; fish)
ش	shiin (sh)	*sheen*	Sounds like the "sh" in "sheep"	shams (*shah-mes*; sun)
ص	Saad (S)	*sahd*	A very deep "s" sound you can make if you open your mouth really wide and lower your jaw	Sadiiq (*sah-deek*; friend)
ض	Daad (D)	*dahd*	A very deep "d" sound; the exact same sound as a Saad except that you use a "d" instead of an "s"	Dabaab (*dah-bahb*; fog)
ط	Taa' (T)	*tah*	A deep "t" sound; start off by saying a regular "t" and then lower your mouth to make it rounder	Tabiib (*tah-beeb*; doctor)
ظ	DHaa' (DH)	*dhah*	Take the "th" as in "those" and draw it to the back of your throat	DHahr (*dha-her*; back)

Arabic Character	Name of the Letter	Pronun-ciation	Sounds Like...	Example
ع	'ayn (')	*ayen*	No equivalent in any of the Romance languages; produced at the very back of the throat. Breathe heavily and consistently through your esophagus and then intermit-tently choke off the airflow so that you create a staccato noise	iraaq (*ee-rahk;* Iraq)
غ	ghayn (gh)	*ghayen*	Sounds like the French "r" in "rendezvous"; it's created at the back of the throat	ghariib (*ghah-reeb;* strange)
ف	faa' (f)	*fah*	Sounds like the "f" in "Frank"	funduq (*foon-dook;* hotel)
ق	qaaf (q)	*qahf*	Similar to the letter "k," but produced much farther at the back of the throat; you should feel airflow being constricted at the back of your throat	qahwa (*qah-wah;* coffee)
ك	kaaf (k)	*kahf*	Sounds like the "k" in "keeper"	kutub (*koo-toob;* books)

(continued)

Table 1-3 *(continued)*

Arabic Character	Name of the Letter	Pronun-ciation	Sounds Like . . .	Example
ل	laam (l)	*lahm*	Sounds like the "l" in "llama"	lisaan (*lee-sahn*; tongue)
م	miim (m)	*meem*	Sounds like the "m" in "Mary"	Makhzan (*mah-khzan*; storehouse)
ن	nuun (n)	*noon*	Sounds like the "n" in "no"	naDHiif (*nah-dheef*; clean)
ه	haa' (h)	*haah*	Created by exhaling heavily; very different from the Haa' earlier in the list. (Think of yourself as a marathon runner who's just finished a long race and is breathing heavily through the lungs to replenish your oxygen.)	huwa (*hoo-wah*; him)
و	waaw (w)	*wahw*	Sounds like the "w" in "winner"	waziir (*wah-zeer*; minister)
ي	yaa' (y)	*yaah*	Sounds like the "y" in "yes"	yamiin (*yah-meen*; right)

To sound as fluent as possible, memorize as many of the letters as you can and try to associate each letter with the Arabic words in which it appears. The trick to getting the pronunciation of some of the more exotic Arabic sounds is repetition, repetition, and even more repetition!

Tackling Tough Letters and Words

In this section, I help you focus on pronunciation of difficult letters. Here are some difficult letters and some related words you should familiarize yourself with:

- ✔ **Haa': Hamraa'** (*hahm-raah;* red); **Hassan** (*hah-san;* man's name); **Hiwaar** (*hee-war;* conversation); **Haziin** (*hah-zeen;* sad)

- ✔ **'ayn: 'ajiib** (*ah-jeeb;* amazing); **'aziima** (*ah-zee-mah;* determination); **'ariiD** (*ah-reed;* wide)

- ✔ **qaaf: qif** (*kee-f;* stop); **qird** (*kee-red;* monkey); **qaws** (*qah-wes;* bow)

- ✔ **ghayn: ghaDbaan** (*ghad-bahn;* angry); **ghurfa** (*ghoor-fah;* room); **ghadan** (*ghah-dan;* tomorrow)

The difference between native Arabic speakers and nonnatives is enunciation. So your challenge is to enunciate your letters clearly — particularly the more difficult ones. Practice these words over and over until you feel comfortable repeating them quickly and distinctly.

Addressing Arabic Transcription

The transcription I use in this book is a widely used and universally recognized method of transcribing Arabic to English. Students of Arabic across the United States and around the world use this method. It's very helpful for beginners because it allows you to speak the language without actually knowing how to read Arabic script.

In the transcription method used in this book, every letter in Arabic is represented by a letter in Roman script. It's important to note that this method is case-sensitive, which means that a lowercase Roman letter represents a different letter in the Arabic script than a capital Roman letter.

Transcription is a very helpful tool for beginners, but it's recommended that intermediate and advanced students of Arabic master the fundamentals of the Arabic script.

Chapter 2

Grammar on a Diet: Just the Basics

- -

In This Chapter

▶ Playing around with nouns and adjectives

▶ Using definite and indefinite articles

▶ Forming simple sentences

▶ Getting to know Arabic verbs

- -

*G*rammar is the glue that binds all the different elements of language together and allows us to communicate using a defined set of rules. This chapter gives you the most important of those rules.

Introducing Nouns, Adjectives, and Articles

Nouns name a person, place, thing, quality, or action. Adjectives modify nouns. Although nouns and adjectives go hand in hand, the best way to understand how they work in Arabic is to address each one separately.

Getting a grip on nouns

In Arabic, every noun has a masculine, feminine, singular, and plural form. Table 2-1 lists some common Arabic nouns. You'll notice that I've listed both singular and plural forms of some nouns, as well as masculine (M) and feminine (F) forms of others.

Table 2-1	Common Nouns in Arabic	
Arabic	**Pronunciation**	**Translation**
walad	*wah-lad*	boy
'awlaad	*aw-lad*	boys
bint	*bee-net*	girl
banaat	*bah-nat*	girls
tilmiidh	*teel-meez*	student (M)
tilmiidha	*teel-mee-zah*	student (F)
mudarris	*moo-dah-rees*	teacher (M)
mudarrisa	*moo-dah-ree-sah*	teacher (F)
kitaab	*kee-tab*	book
Taawila	*tah-wee-lah*	table
sayyaara	*sah-yah-rah*	car

Identifying adjectives

In Arabic, an adjective must be in agreement with the noun it modifies in both gender and plurality. Table 2-2 presents some common adjectives in both the feminine and masculine forms.

Table 2-2	Common Adjectives in Arabic	
Arabic	**Pronunciation**	**Translation**
kabiir	*kah-beer*	big (M)
kabiira	*kah-bee-rah*	big (F)

Arabic	Pronunciation	Translation
Saghiir	sah-gheer	small (M)
Saghiira	sah-ghee-rah	small (F)
Tawiil	tah-weel	tall (M)
Tawiila	tah-wee-lah	tall (F)
qaSiir	qah-seer	short (M)
qaSiira	qah-see-rah	short (F)
jamiil	jah-meel	beautiful/handsome (M)
jamiila	jah-mee-lah	beautiful/pretty (F)

Notice that all you do is add the suffix **-a** to the masculine adjective to obtain its feminine form. This rule applies to all regular adjective forms.

One of the biggest differences between adjective and noun interactions in the English and Arabic languages is that nouns in Arabic come *before* the adjectives. In English, nouns always come *after* their adjectives.

Discovering definite and indefinite articles (and the sun and moon)

A common trait that nouns and adjectives share in the Arabic language is that both can be modified using definite article prefixes. To refresh your memory, an *article* is a part of speech that you use to indicate nouns or adjectives and specify their applications. In English, there are two types of articles: indefinite and definite. The indefinite articles in English

are "a" and "an," such as in "a book" or "an umbrella."
The definite article is the word "the," as in "the book"
or "the umbrella."

Unlike English, Arabic has no outright indefinite
article; instead, the indefinite article in Arabic is
always implied. For example, when you say **kitaab**
(*kee-tab;* book), you mean both "book" and "a book."
Similarly, **madrasa** (*mad-rah-sah;* school) means
both "school" and "a school." However, Arabic does
employ a definite article, which is the prefix you
attach to either the noun or the adjective you want
to define.

The rule

The definite article in Arabic is the prefix **al-.**
When you want to define a noun or adjective,
you simply attach this prefix to the word. For
example, "the book" is **al-kitaab,** and "the school"
is **al-madrasa.**

The inevitable exceptions

Sometimes, the "l" in the prefix **al-** drops off
and is replaced by a letter identical to the
first letter of the word being defined. For
example, the word **nuur** (*noor*) means
"light" in Arabic. If you want to say "the
light," you say **an-nuur** (*ah-noor*), replacing
the "l" in **al-** with the first letter of the definite word.

So how do you know whether to use **al-** or another
definite article prefix format? The answer's really
cool. Every single letter in Arabic falls into one of
two categories: sun letters and moon letters. Every
word that begins with a moon letter gets the prefix
al-, and every word that begins with a sun letter
gets the prefix **a-** followed by its sun letter. Table 2-3
lists all the sun letters. Every other letter in Arabic
is automatically a moon letter.

Table 2-3	The Sun Letters	
Arabic	*Pronunciation*	*Translation*
ت	*taa*	t
ث	*thaa*	th
د	*daal*	d
ذ	*dhaal*	dh
ر	*raa*	r
ز	*zay*	z
س	*siin*	s
ش	*shiin*	sh
ص	*Saad*	S
ض	*Daad*	D
ط	*Taa*	T
ظ	*Dhaa*	DH
ن	*nuun*	n

Understanding the interaction between nouns and adjectives

In Arabic, the way you pair up nouns and adjectives creates definite and indefinite phrases.

Indefinite phrases

To create an indefinite phrase, all you do is take an undefined noun and add to it an undefined adjective. For example, to say "a big book" or "big book," you add the adjective **kabiir** (*kah-beer;* big) to the noun **kitaab** (*kee-tab;* book). So the phrase **kitaab kabiir** means "a big book" in Arabic. Here are some other examples:

✔ **walad Tawiil** (*wah-lad tah-weel;* a tall boy)

✔ **bint jamiila** (*bee-net jah-mee-lah;* a pretty girl)

✔ **Taawila Hamraa'** (*tah-wee-lah ham-rah;* a red table)

Adding more descriptive words to the noun is very simple: Because adjectives follow the noun in Arabic, you just add an extra adjective and you're done! But don't forget to add the conjunction **wa** (*wah;* and) between the adjectives. Check out some examples:

- ✔ **walad Tawiil wa kabiir** (*wah-lad tah-weel wah kah-beer;* a tall and big boy)

- ✔ **bint Tawiila wa jamiila** (*bee-net tah-wee-lah wah jah-mee-lah;* a tall and pretty girl)

- ✔ **Taawila Hamraa' wa qaSiira** (*tah-wee-lah ham-rah wah qah-see-rah;* a red and short table)

Definite phrases

The biggest difference between creating an indefinite phrase and a definite phrase is the use of the definite article prefix **al-**. Both noun and adjective must be defined using the definite article prefix. For example, to say "the big book," you say **al-kitaab al-kabiir.** Here are some examples of definite phrases:

- ✔ **al-walad aT-Tawiil** (*al-wah-lad ah-tah-weel;* the big boy)

- ✔ **al-bint al-jamiila** (*al-bee-net al-jah-mee-lah;* the pretty girl)

- ✔ **aT-Taawila al-Hamraa'** (*ah-tah-wee-lah al-ham-rah;* the red table)

Using similar patterns, you can create a defined phrase using multiple adjectives. Just like in indefinite phrases, make sure you use the conjunction **wa** between adjectives:

- ✔ **al-walad aT-Tawiil wa al-kabiir** (*al-wah-lad ah-tah-weel wah al-kah-beer;* the tall and big boy)

- ✔ **al-bint aT-Tawiila wa al-jamiila** (*al-bee-net ah-tah-wee-lah wah al-jah-mee-lah;* the tall and pretty girl)

- ✔ **aT-Taawila al-Hamraa' wa al-qaSiira** (*ah-tah-wee-lah al-ham-rah wah al-qah-see-rah;* the red and short table)

Creating Simple, Verb-Free Sentences

There are two ways to form sentences in Arabic: You can manipulate definite and indefinite nouns and adjectives, or you can pull together nouns, adjectives, and verbs.

To be or not to be: Sentences without verbs

There's actually no "to be" verb in the Arabic language. You create "to be" sentences by manipulating indefinite and definite nouns and adjectives.

When you put an indefinite noun with an indefinite adjective, you create an indefinite phrase. Similarly, when you add a definite adjective to a definite noun, you end up with a definite phrase. So what happens when you combine a definite noun with an indefinite adjective? This combination — defined noun and undefined adjective — produces an "is/are" sentence similar to what you get when you use the verb "to be" in English.

Take the defined noun **al-kitaab** (the book) and add to it the indefinite adjective **kabiir** (big). The resulting phrase is **al-kitaab kabiir,** which means "The book is big." Here are some more examples to illustrate the construction of "is/are" sentences:

- ✔ **as-sayyaara khadraa'.** (*ah-sah-yah-rah kad-rah;* The car is green.)
- ✔ **aT-Taaliba dakiiya.** (*ah-tah-lee-bah dah-kee-yah;* The student is smart.) (F)
- ✔ **al-'ustaadh Tawiil.** (*al-oos-taz tah-weel;* The professor is tall.) (M)

If you want to use additional adjectives in these verb-free sentences, you simply add the conjunction **wa**. Here are some examples of "is/are" sentences with multiple adjectives:

✔ **as-sayyaara khadraa' wa sarii'a.** (*ah-sah-yah-rah kad-rah wah sah-ree-ah;* The car is green and fast.)

✔ **aT-Taaliba dakiiya wa laTiifa.** (*ah-tah-lee-bah dah-kee-yah wah lah-tee-fah;* The student is smart and nice.) (F)

✔ **al-'ustaadh Tawiil wa Sa'b.** (*al-oos-taz tah-weel wah sahb;* The professor is tall and difficult.) (M)

This construct is fairly flexible, and if you change the nature of one of the adjectives, you radically alter the meaning of the **jumla** (*joom-lah;* sentence). For instance, the examples all show a defined noun with two indefinite adjectives. What happens when you mix things up and add an indefinite noun to an indefinite adjective and a definite adjective?

Consider the example **al-bint SaHiiHa wa qawiiya** (The girl is healthy and strong). Keep **al-bint** as a definite noun but change the indefinite adjective **SaHiiHa** into its definite version, **aS-SaHiiHa;** also, drop the **wa,** and keep **qawiiya** as an indefinite adjective. The resulting phrase is **al-bint aS-SaHiiHa qawiiya,** which means "The healthy girl is strong."

You can grasp what's going on here by dividing the terms into clauses: The first clause is the definite noun/definite adjective combination **al-bint aS-SaHiiHa** (the healthy girl); the second clause is the indefinite adjective **qawiiya** (strong). Combining these clauses is the same as combining a definite noun with an indefinite adjective — the result is an "is/are" sentence. Here are more examples to help clear up any confusion regarding this concept:

✔ **as-sayyaara al-khadraa' sarii'a.** (*ah-sah-yah-rah al-kad-rah sah-ree-ah;* The green car is fast.)

✔ **aT-Taaliba ad-dhakiiya laTiifa.** (*ah-tah-lee-bah ah-dhah-kee-yah lah-tee-fah;* The smart student is nice.) (F)

✔ **al-'ustaadh aT-Tawiil Sa'b.** (*al-oos-taz ah-tah-weel sahb;* The tall professor is difficult.) (M)

Building sentences with common prepositions

Prepositions indicate a relationship between substantive and other types of words, such as adjectives, verbs, nouns, or other substantives. Table 2-4 lists the most common prepositions you're likely to use in Arabic.

Table 2-4	Common Prepositions	
Arabic	*Pronunciation*	*Translation*
min	*meen*	from
fii	*fee*	in
'ilaa	*ee-lah*	to
ma'a	*mah-ah*	with
'alaa	*ah-lah*	on
qariib min	*qah-reeb meen*	close to
ba'iid min	*bah-eed meen*	far from
'amaama	*ah-mah-mah*	in front of
waraa'a	*wah-rah-ah*	behind
taHta	*tah-tah*	underneath
fawqa	*faw-qah*	above
bijaanibi	*bee-jah-nee-bee*	next to

You can use these prepositions to construct clauses and phrases using both indefinite and definite nouns and adjectives. Here are some examples:

- ✔ **al-'ustaadha fii al-jaami'a.** (*al-oos-tah-zah fee al-jah-mee-ah;* The professor is in the university.) (F)

- ✔ **al-maT'am bijaanibi al-funduq.** (*al-mat-ham bee-jah-nee-bee al-foon-dook;* The restaurant is next to the hotel.)

✔ **as-sayyaara al-bayDaa' waraa'a al-manzil.** (*ah-sah-yah-rah al-bay-dah wah-rah-ah al-man-zeel;* The white car is behind the house.)

✔ **al-walad al-laTiif ma'a al-mudarris.** (*al-wah-lad ah-lah-teef mah-ah al-moo-dah-rees;* The nice boy is with the teacher.)

In addition, you can use multiple adjectives with both the subject and object nouns:

✔ **al-'imra'a al-jamiila fii as-sayyaara as-sarii'a.** (*al-eem-rah-ah al-jah-mee-lah fee ah-sah-yah-rah ah-sah-ree-ah;* The beautiful woman is in the fast car.)

✔ **al-mudarissa ad-dakiyya 'amaama al-madrasa al-bayDaa'.** (*al-moo-dah-ree-sah ah-dah-kee-yah ah-mah-mah al-mad-rah-sah al-bay-dah;* The smart teacher is in front of the white school.) (F)

✔ **al-kursiiy aS-Saghiir waraa'a aT-Taawila al-kabiira.** (*al-koor-see ah-sah-gheer wah-rah-ah ah-tah-wee-lah al-kah-bee-rah;* The small chair is behind the big table.)

Using demonstratives and forming sentences

A *demonstrative* indicates the noun that you're referring to. Common demonstratives in English are the words "this" and "that." If a demonstrative refers to a number of objects (such as "those" or "these"), it's gender-neutral and may be used for both masculine and feminine objects. If you're using a singular demonstrative ("this" or "that"), it must agree with the gender of the object being singled out.

Following are demonstratives in the singular format:

✔ **haadhaa** (*hah-zah;* this) (M)
✔ **haadhihi** (*hah-zee-hee;* this) (F)
✔ **dhaalika** (*zah-lee-kah;* that) (M)
✔ **tilka** (*teel-kah;* that) (F)

Here are the plural demonstratives, which are gender-neutral:

- ✔ **haa'ulaa'i** (*hah-oo-lah-ee;* these)
- ✔ **'ulaa'ika** (*oo-lah-ee-kah;* those)

You can combine demonstratives with both definite and indefinite nouns and adjectives. For example, to say "this boy," add the definite noun **al-walad** (boy) to the demonstrative **haadhaa** (this; M); because demonstratives always come before the nouns they identify, the resulting phrase is **haadhaa al-walad.** Here are more examples of this construct:

- ✔ **haadhihi al-bint** (*hah-zee-hee al-bee-net;* this girl)
- ✔ **'ulaa'ika al-banaat** (*oo-lah-ee-kah al-bah-nat;* those girls)
- ✔ **haa'ulaa'i al-'awlaad** (*hah-oo-lah-ee al-aw-lad;* these boys)
- ✔ **tilka al-'ustaadha** (*teel-kah al-oos-tah-zah;* that professor) (F)
- ✔ **dhaalika al-kitaab** (*zah-lee-kah al-kee-tab;* that book)

When a demonstrative is followed by a defined noun, you get a definite clause, as in the examples in the preceding list. However, when you attach an indefinite noun to a demonstrative, the result is an "is/are" sentence. For instance, if you add the demonstrative **haadhaa** to the indefinite subject noun **walad**, you get **haadhaa walad** (*hah-zah wah-lad;* This is a boy). Using the examples from the preceding list, I show you what happens when you drop the definite article from the subject noun in a demonstrative clause:

- ✔ **haadhihi bint.** (*hah-zee-hee bee-net;* This is a girl.)
- ✔ **'ulaa'ika banaat.** (*oo-lah-ee-kah bah-nat;* Those are girls.)

- ✔ **haa'ulaa'i 'awlaad.** (*hah-oo-lah-ee aw-lad;* These are boys.)
- ✔ **tilka 'ustaadha.** (*teel-kah oos-tah-zah;* That is a professor.) (F)
- ✔ **dhaalika kitaab.** (*zah-lee-kah kee-tab;* That is a book.)

When you combine a demonstrative clause with a definite subject noun and an indefinite adjective, the resulting phrase is a more descriptive "is/are" sentence:

- ✔ **haadhihi al-bint jamiila.** (*hah-zee-hee al-bee-net jah-mee-lah;* This girl is pretty.)
- ✔ **'ulaa'ika al-banaat Tawiilaat.** (*oo-lah-ee-kah al-bah-nat tah-wee-lat;* Those girls are tall.)
- ✔ **tilka al-madrasa kabiira.** (*teel-kah al-mad-rah-sah kah-bee-rah;* That school is big.)

Conversely, when you combine a demonstrative clause with a definite subject noun and a definite adjective, you get a regular demonstrative phrase:

- ✔ **haadhaa ar-rajul al-jamiil** (*hah-zah ah-rah-jool al-jah-meel;* that handsome man)
- ✔ **dhaalika al-kitaab al-'ajiib** (*zah-lee-kah al-kee-tab al-ah-jeeb;* that amazing book)
- ✔ **tilka al-madiina aS-Saghiira** (*teel-kah al-mah-dee-nah ah-sah-ghee-rah;* that small city)

Forming "to be" sentences using personal pronouns

Personal pronouns stand in for people, places, things, or ideas. Table 2-5 presents all the major personal pronouns in the Arabic language.

In the translation and conjugation tables in this section and throughout this book, in addition to singular and plural denotations, you see a form labeled *dual*. This number form doesn't exist in English. It is reserved for describing two items (no more, no less).

Table 2-5	**Personal Pronouns**	
Arabic	*Pronunciation*	*Translation*
'anaa	*ah-nah*	I/me
'anta	*an-tah*	you (MS)
'anti	*an-tee*	you (FS)
huwa	*hoo-wah*	he/it
hiya	*hee-yah*	she/it
naHnu	*nah-noo*	we
'antum	*an-toom*	you (MP)
'antunna	*an-too-nah*	you (FP)
hum	*hoom*	they (MP)
hunna	*hoo-nah*	they (FP)
'antumaa	*an-too-mah*	you (dual)
humaa	*hoo-mah*	they (M/dual)
humaa	*hoo-mah*	they (F/dual)

The personal pronoun always comes before the predicate noun that it designates, and it also creates an "is/are" sentence. For instance, when you say **hiya bint** (*hee-yah bee-net*), you mean "She is a girl." Similarly, **huwa walad** (*hoo-wah wah-lad*) means "He is a boy." The meaning changes slightly when the subject noun is defined. For example, **hiya al-bint** means "She is the girl," and **huwa al-walad** means "He is the boy." Here are some more examples:

✔ **'anaa rajul.** (*ah-nah rah-jool;* I am a man.)

✔ **'anaa ar-rajul.** (*ah-nah ah-rah-jool;* I am the man.)

✔ **hum 'awlaad.** (*hoom aw-lad;* They are boys.)

✔ **hiya al-'imra'a.** (*hee-yah al-eem-rah-ah;* She is the woman.)

✔ **'anta kabiir.** (*an-tah kah-beer;* You are big.) (MS)

✔ **'anti jamiila.** (*an-tee jah-mee-lah;* You are beautiful.) (FS)

✔ **'antum su'adaa'.** (*an-toom soo-ah-dah;* You are happy.) (MP)

✔ **'anti bint jamiila.** (*an-tee bee-net jah-mee-lah;* You are a pretty girl.)

✔ **'anta al-walad al-kabiir.** (*an-tah al-wah-lad al-kah-beer;* You are the big boy.)

✔ **hunna 'an-nisaa' al-laTiifaat.** (*hoo-nah ah-nee-sah ah-lah-tee-fat;* They are the nice women.)

✔ **hunna nisaa' laTiifaat.** (*hoo-nah nee-sah lah-tee-fat;* They are nice women.)

✔ **huwa rajul qawiiy.** (*hoo-wah rah-jool qah-wee;* He is a strong man.)

✔ **huwa ar-rajul al-qawiiy.** (*hoo-wah ah-rah-jool al-qah-wee;* He is the strong man.)

Creating negative "to be" sentences

Although Arabic doesn't have a "to be" regular verb to create "I am" or "you are" phrases, it does have a verb you use to say "I am not" or "you are not." This special irregular verb **laysa** (*lay-sah*) creates negative "to be" sentences. Table 2-6 shows **laysa** conjugated using all the personal pronouns.

Table 2-6	The Present Tense of the Verb *laysa* (Not To Be)	
Form	**Pronunciation**	**Translation**
'anaa lastu	*ah-nah las-too*	I am not
'anta lasta	*an-tah las-tah*	You are not (MS)
'anti lasti	*an-tee las-tee*	You are not (FS)
huwa laysa	*hoo-wah lay-sah*	He is not
hiya laysat	*hee-yah lay-sat*	She is not
naHnu lasnaa	*nah-noo las-nah*	We are not
'antum lastum	*an-toom las-toom*	You are not (MP)
'antunna lastunna	*an-too-nah las-too-nah*	You are not (FP)
hum laysuu	*hoom lay-soo*	They are not (MP)
hunna lasna	*hoo-nah las-nah*	They are not (FP)
antumaa lastu-maa	*an-too-mah las-too-mah*	You are not (dual/MP/FP)
humaa laysaa	*hoo-mah lay-sah*	They are not (dual/MP)
humaa laysataa	*hoo-mah lay-sah-tah*	They are not (dual/FP)

Following are some examples of negative "to be" sentences using the verb **laysa**:

- ✔ **'anaa lastu Taalib.** (*ah-nah las-too tah-leeb;* I am not a student.)

- ✔ **'anta lasta mariiD.** (*an-tah las-tah mah-reed;* You are not sick.) (M)

- ✔ **naHnu lasnaa fii al-madrasa.** (*nah-noo las-nah fee al-mad-rah-sah;* We are not in the school.)

- ✔ **al-bint aT-Tawiila laysat Da'iifa.** (*al-bee-net ah-tah-wee-lah lay-sat dah-ee-fah;* The tall girl is not weak.)

"To be" in the past tense

Arabic's verb for "was/were" (in other words, "to be" in the past tense) is **kaana** (*kah-nah;* was/were). Similar to the negative form of "to be," the past form is an irregular verb form conjugated using all the personal pronouns. See Table 2-7.

Table 2-7	The Past Tense of the Verb *kaana* (Was/Were)	
Form	*Pronunciation*	*Translation*
'anaa kuntu	*ah-nah koon-too*	I was
'anta kunta	*an-tah koon-tah*	You were (MS)
'anti kunti	*an-tee koon-tee*	You were (FS)
huwa kaana	*hoo-wah kah-nah*	He was
hiya kaanat	*hee-yah kah-nat*	She was
naHnu kunnaa	*nah-noo koo-nah*	We were
'antum kuntum	*an-toom koon-toom*	You were (MP)
'antunna kuntunna	*an-too-nah koon-too-nah*	You were (FP)
hum kaanuu	*hoom kah-noo*	They were (MP)
hunna kunna	*hoo-nah koo-nah*	They were (FP)
antumaa kuntumaa	*an-too-mah koon-too-mah*	You were (dual/MP/FP)
humaa kaanaa	*hoo-mah kah-nah*	They were (dual/MP)
humaa kaanataa	*hoo-mah kah-nah-tah*	They were (dual/FP)

Here are some sentences featuring **kaana**:

✔ **'anaa kuntu mariiD.** (*ah-nah koon-too mah-reed;* I was sick.)

✔ **'anta kunta fii al-maktaba.** (*an-tah koon-tah fee al-mak-tah-bah;* You were in the library.)

> ✔ **hiya kaanat qariiba min al-manzil.** (*hee-yah kah-nat qah-ree-bah meen al-man-zeel;* She was close to the house.)
>
> ✔ **naHnu kunnaa fii al-masbaH.** (*nah-noo koo-nah fee al-mas-bah;* We were in the swimming pool.)
>
> ✔ **al-'imra'a wa ar-rajul kaanaa fii al-Hubb.** (*al-eem-rah-ah wah ah-rah-jool kah-nah fee al-hoob;* The woman and the man were in love.)

Working with Verbs

Verb tenses in Arabic are fairly straightforward. Basically, you need to be concerned with only two proper verb forms: the past and the present. A future verb tense exists, but it's a derivative of the present tense that you achieve by attaching a prefix to the present tense of the verb.

Digging up the past tense

The structural form of the past tense is one of the easiest grammatical structures in the Arabic language. First, you refer to all regular verbs in the past tense using the **huwa** (*hoo-wah;* he) personal pronoun. Second, the overwhelming majority of verbs in **huwa** form in the past tense have three consonants that are accompanied by the same vowel: the **fatHa** (*feht-hah*). The **fatHa** creates the "ah" sound.

For example, the verb "wrote" in the past tense is **kataba** (*kah-tah-bah*); its three consonants are "k," "t," and "b." Here are some common verbs you may use while speaking Arabic:

> ✔ **'akala** (*ah-kah-lah;* ate)
>
> ✔ **fa'ala** (*fah-ah-lah;* did)
>
> ✔ **ra'a** (*rah-ah;* saw)

Table 2-8 shows the verb **kataba** (*kah-tah-bah;* wrote) conjugated using all the personal pronouns. Note that the first part of the verb remains constant; only its suffix changes depending on the personal pronoun used.

Table 2-8	The Past Tense of the Verb *kataba* (To Write)	
Form	*Pronunciation*	*Translation*
'anaa katabtu	*ah-nah kah-tab-too*	I wrote
'anta katabta	*an-tah kah-tab-tah*	You wrote (MS)
'anti katabtii	*an-tee kah-tab-tee*	You wrote (FS)
huwa kataba	*hoo-wah kah-tah-bah*	He wrote
hiya katabat	*hee-yah kah-tah-bat*	She wrote
naHnu katabnaa	*nah-noo kah-tab-nah*	We wrote
'antum katabtum	*an-toom kah-tab-toom*	You wrote (MP)
'antunna katabtunna	*an-too-nah kah-tab-too-nah*	You wrote (FP)
hum katabuu	*hoom kah-tah-boo*	They wrote (MP)
hunna katabna	*hoo-nah kah-tab-nah*	They wrote (FP)
antumaa katabtumaa	*an-too-mah kah-tab-too-mah*	You wrote (dual/M./FP)
humaa katabaa	*hoo-mah kah-tah-bah*	They wrote (dual/MP)
humaa katabataa	*hoo-mah kah-tah-bah-tah*	They wrote (dual/FP)

Every personal pronoun has a corresponding suffix used to conjugate and identify the verb form in its specific tense. Table 2-9 outlines these specific suffixes.

Table 2-9	Personal Pronoun Suffixes for Verbs in the Past Tense		
Arabic Pronoun	*Pronunciation*	*Translation*	*Verb Suffix*
'anaa	*ah-nah*	I/me	**-tu**
'anta	*an-tah*	you (MS)	**-ta**
'anti	*an-tee*	you (FS)	**-tii**
huwa	*hoo-wah*	he/it	**-a**
hiya	*hee-yah*	she/it	**-at**
naHnu	*nah-noo*	we	**-naa**
'antum	*an-toom*	you (MP)	**-tum**
'antunna	*an-too-nah*	you (FP)	**tunna**
hum	*hoom*	they (MP)	**-uu**
hunna	*hoo-nah*	they (FP)	**-na**
'antumaa	*an-too-mah*	you (dual)	**tumaaa**
humaa	*hoo-mah*	they (M/dual)	**-aa**
humaa	*hoo-mah*	they (F/dual)	**-ataa**

Anytime you come across a regular verb you want to conjugate in the past tense, use these verb suffixes with the corresponding personal pronouns.

Here are some simple sentences that combine nouns, adjectives, and verbs in the past tense:

- ✔ **'al-walad dhahaba 'ilaa al-madrasa.** (*al-wah-lad zah-hah-bah ee-lah al-mad-rah-sah;* The boy went to the school.)

- ✔ **'akalnaa Ta'aam ladhiidh.** (*ah-kal-nah tah-am lah-zeez;* We ate delicious food.)

- ✔ **dhahaba ar-rajul 'ilaa al-jaami'a fii as-sayaara.** (*zah-hah-bah ah-rah-jool ee-lah al-jah-mee-ah fee ah-sah-yah-rah;* The man went to the school in the car.)

Note that some regular verbs have more than three consonants, such as:

▶ **tafarraja** (*tah-fah-rah-jah;* watched)

▶ **takallama** (*tah-kah-lah-mah;* spoke)

To conjugate them, you keep the first part of the word constant and change only the last part of the word using the corresponding suffixes to match the personal pronouns.

Examining the present tense

Conjugating verbs in the present tense is a bit trickier. Instead of changing only the ending of the verb, you must also alter its beginning.

To illustrate the difference between past and present tense, Table 2-10 conjugates the verb **kataba** (wrote) as **yaktubu** (*yak-too-boo;* to write).

Table 2-10	The Present Tense of the Verb *yaktubu* (To Write)	
Form	*Pronunciation*	*Translation*
'anaa 'aktubu	*ah-nah ak-too-boo*	I am writing
'anta taktubu	*an-tah tak-too-boo*	You are writing (MS)
'anti taktubiina	*an-tee tak-too-bee-nah*	You are writing (FS)
huwa yaktubu	*hoo-wah yak-too-boo*	He is writing
hiya taktubu	*hee-yah tak-too-boo*	She is writing
naHnu naktubu	*nah-noo nak-too-boo*	We are writing
'antum taktubuuna	*an-toom tak-too-boo-nah*	You are writing (MP)

Form	Pronunciation	Translation
'antunna taktubna	*an-too-nah tak-toob-nah*	You are writing (FP)
hum yaktubuuna	*hoom yak-too-boo-nah*	They are writing (MP)
hunna yaktubna	*hoo-nah yak-toob-nah*	They are writing (FP)
antumaa taktubaani	*an-too-mah tak-too-bah-nee*	You are writing (dual/MP/FP)
humaa yaktubaani	*hoo-mah yak-too-bah-nee*	They are writing (dual/MP)
humaa taktubaani	*hoo-mah tak-too-bah-nee*	They are writing (dual/FP)

As you can see, you need to be familiar with both the prefixes and suffixes to conjugate verbs in the present tense. Table 2-11 includes every personal pronoun with its corresponding prefix and suffix for the present tense.

Table 2-11   Personal Pronoun Prefixes and Suffixes for Verbs in the Present Tense

Arabic Pronoun	Pronunciation	Translation	Verb Prefix	Verb Suffix
'anaa	*ah-nah*	I/me	**'a-**	**-u**
'anta	*an-tah*	you (MS)	**ta-**	**-u**
'anti	*an-tee*	you (FS)	**ta-**	**-iina**
huwa	*hoo-wah*	he/it	**ya-**	**-u**
hiya	*hee-yah*	she/it	**ta-**	**-u**

(continued)

Table 2-11 *(continued)*

Arabic Pronoun	Pronunciation	Translation	Verb Prefix	Verb Suffix
naHnu	*nah-noo*	we	**na-**	**-u**
'antum	*an-toom*	you (MP)	**ta-**	**-uuna**
'antunna	*an-too-nah*	you (FP)	**ta-**	**-na**
hum	*hoom*	they (MP)	**ya-**	**-uuna**
hunna	*hoo-nah*	they (FP)	**ya-**	**-na**
'antumaa	*an-too-mah*	you (dual)	**ta-**	**-aani**
humaa	*hoo-mah*	they (M/ dual)	**ya-**	**-aani**
humaa	*hoo-mah*	they (F/dual)	**ta-**	**-aani**

Aside from prefixes and suffixes, another major difference between the past and present tenses in Arabic is that every verb in the present tense has a dominant vowel that's unique and distinctive. For example, the dominant vowel in **yaktubu** is a **damma** (*dah-mah;* "ooh" sound). However, in the verb **yaf'alu** (*yaf-ahloo;* to do), the dominant vowel is the **fatHa** (*feht-hah;* "ah" sound). This means that when you conjugate the verb **saf'alu** using the personal pronoun **'anaa,** you say **'anaa 'af'alu** and *not* **'anaa 'af'ulu.** For complete coverage of Arabic vowels (**damma, fatHa,** and **kasra**), check out Chapter 1.

The dominant vowel is always the middle vowel. Unfortunately, there's no hard rule you can use to determine which dominant vowel is associated with each verb. The best way to identify the dominant vowel is to look up the verb in the **qaamuus** (*qahmoos;* dictionary).

In this list, I divide up some of the most common Arabic verbs according to their dominant vowels:

damma

- **yaktubu** (*yak-too-boo;* to write)
- **yadrusu** (*yad-roo-soo;* to study)
- **ya'kulu** (*yah-koo-loo;* to eat)
- **yaskunu** (*yas-koo-noo;* to live)

fatHa

- **yaf'alu** (*yaf-ah-loo;* to do)
- **yaqra'u** (*yak-rah-oo;* to read)
- **yadhhabu** (*yaz-hah-boo;* to go)
- **yaftaHu** (*yaf-tah-hoo;* to open)

kasra

- **yarji'u** (*yar-jee-oo;* to return)
- **ya'rifu** (*yah-ree-foo;* to know)

When you conjugate a verb in the present tense, you must do two things:

1. **Identify the dominant vowel that will be used to conjugate the verb using all personal pronouns.**

2. **Isolate the prefix and suffix that correspond to the appropriate personal pronoun.**

Peeking into the future tense

You achieve the future tense by adding the prefix **sa-** to the existing present tense form of the verb. For example, **yaktubu** means "to write." Add the prefix **sa-** to **yaktubu** and you get **sayaktubu,** which means "he will write." Table 2-12 shows how to conjugate this verb.

Table 2-12	The Future Tense of the Verb *sayaktubu* (To Write)	
Form	*Pronunciation*	*Translation*
'anaa sa'aktubu	*ah-nah sah-ak-too-boo*	I will write
'anta sataktubu	*an-tah sah-tak-too-boo*	You will write (MS)
'anti sataktubiina	*an-tee sah-tak-too-bee-nah*	You will write (FS)
huwa sayaktubu	*hoo-wah sah-yak-too-boo*	He will write
hiya sataktubu	*hee-yah sah-tak-too-boo*	She will write
naHnu sanaktubu	*nah-noo sah-nak-too-boo*	We will write
'antum sataktubuuna	*an-toom sah-tak-too-boo-nah*	You will write (MP)
'antunna sataktubna	*an-too-nah sah-tak-toob-nah*	You will write (FP)
hum sayaktubuuna	*hoom sah-yak-too-boo-nah*	They will write (MP)
hunna sayaktubna	*hoo-nah sah-yak-toob-nah*	They will write (FP)
antumaa sataktubaani	*an-too-mah sah-tak-too-bah-nee*	You will write (dual/MP/FP)
humaa sayaktubaani	*hoo-mah sah-yak-too-bah-nee*	They will write (dual/MP)
humaa sataktubaani	*hoo-mah sah-tak-too-bah-nee*	They will write (dual/FP)

Chapter 3

Numerical Gumbo: Counting of All Kinds

- -

In This Chapter

▶ Counting to 100

▶ Telling time

▶ Counting the days

▶ Spending money

- -

1n this chapter, I introduce you to the basics of counting in Arabic so you can talk about time, days, money, and more.

Talking Numbers

Arabic **'arqaam** (*ar-qahm;* numbers) are part of one of the earliest traditions of number notation. But even though the Western world's number system is sometimes referred to as "Arabic numerals," actual Arabic **'arqaam** are written differently.

You read Arabic numbers from left to right. That's right! Even though you read and write Arabic from right to left, you read and write Arabic numbers from left to right!

Table 3-1 lays out the Arabic **'arqaam** from 0 to 10.

Table 3-1	Arabic Numerals 0–10	
Arabic	*Pronunciation*	*Translation*
Sifr	*seh-fer*	0
waaHid	*wah-eed*	1
'ithnayn	*eeth-nah-yen*	2
thalaatha	*thah-lah-thah*	3
'arba'a	*ah-reh-bah-ah*	4
khamsa	*khah-meh-sah*	5
sitta	*see-tah*	6
sab'a	*sah-beh-ah*	7
thamaaniya	*thah-mah-nee-yah*	8
tis'a	*tee-seh-ah*	9
'ashra	*ah-she-rah*	10

You get the **'arqaam** from **'iHdaa 'ashar** (11) to **tis'ata 'ashar** (19) by combining a part of **'ashra** (10) — specifically **'ashar** (tenth) — with part of the singular number. In the case of the **'arqaam** from **thalaathata 'ashar** (13) through **tis'ata 'ashar** (19), all you do is add the suffix **-ta** to the regular number and add the derivative form **'ashar.**

Table 3-2 shows the **'arqaam** in increments of 10 from 20 to 100.

Table 3-2	Arabic Numerals 20–100	
Arabic	**Pronunciation**	**Translation**
'ishriin	ee-sheh-reen	20
thalaathiin	thah-lah-theen	30
'arba'iin	ah-reh-bah-een	40
khamsiin	khah-meh-seen	50
sittiin	see-teen	60
sab'iin	sah-beh-een	70
thamaaniin	thah-mah-neen	80
Tis'iin	tee-seh-een	90
Mi'a	mee-ah	100

In English, you add the suffix **-ty** to get thirty, forty, and so on. In Arabic, the suffix **-iin** plays that role, as in **'arba'iin** (40) or **khamsiin** (50).

Discovering Ordinal Numbers

Ordinal numbers are used to order things in a first-second-third kind of format. In Arabic, ordinal numbers are gender-defined, so you need to be familiar with both the masculine and feminine ordinal forms, which I present in Table 3-3.

Table 3-3		Ordinal Numbers		
Ordinal (M)	*Pronunciation*	*Ordinal (F)*	*Pronunciation*	*Translation*
'awwal	*ah-wall*	'uulaa	*ooh-laah*	first
thaanii	*thah-nee*	thaaniya	*thah-nee-yah*	second
thaalith	*thah-leeth*	thaalitha	*thah-lee-thah*	third
raabi'	*rah-bee*	raabi'a	*rah-bee-hah*	fourth
khaamis	*khah-mees*	khaamisa	*khah-mee-sah*	fifth
saadis	*sah-dees*	saadisa	*sah-dee-sah*	sixth
saabi'	*sah-bee*	saabi'a	*sah-bee-ah*	seventh
thaamin	*thah-meen*	thaamina	*thah-meen-ah*	eighth
taasi'	*tah-see*	taasi'a	*tah-see-ah*	ninth
'aashir	*ah-sheer*	'aashira	*ah-shee-rah*	tenth
Haadi 'ashar	*hah-dee ah-shar*	Haadia 'ashra	*hah-dee-yah ash-rah*	eleventh
thaanii 'ashar	*thah-nee ah-shar*	thaaniya 'ashra	*thah-nee-yah ash-rah*	twelfth

Telling Time in Arabic

If you want to ask someone for the time, you ask

kam as-saa'a? (*kam ah-sah-ah;* What time is it?)

If someone asks you this question, answer **as-saa'a** followed by the ordinal of the hour. So you would say, for instance, "It's the eleventh hour" as opposed to saying "It's 11 o'clock." Because **as-saa'a** is a feminine noun, you use the feminine form of the ordinal numbers, which are listed in Table 3-4.

as-saa'a al-Haadiya 'ashra. (*ah-sah-ah al-hah-dee-yah ah-shrah;* It's 11:00.)

Table 3-4	Arabic Ordinals for Telling Time	
Arabic	*Pronunciation*	*Translation*
waaHida	wah-hee-dah	first (F)
thaaniya	thah-nee-yah	second (F)
thaalitha	thah-lee-thah	third (F)
raabi'a	rah-bee-ah	fourth (F)
khaamisa	khah-mee-sah	fifth (F)
saadisa	sah-dee-sah	sixth (F)
saabi'a	sah-bee-ah	seventh (F)
thaamina	thah-mee-nah	eighth (F)
taasi'a	tah-see-ah	ninth (F)
'aashira	ah-shee-rah	tenth (F)
Haadiya 'ashra	hah-dee-yah ah-shrah	eleventh (F)
thaaniya 'ashra	thah-nee-yah ah-shrah	twelfth (F)

You need to use the definite prefix article **al-** with the ordinals because you're referring to a specific hour and not just any hour.

Following are some additional key words related to telling time in Arabic:

- **saa'a** (*sah-ah;* hour)
- **daqiiqa** (*da-kee-qah;* minute)
- **thaaniya** (*thah-nee-yah;* second)
- **ba'da** (*bah-dah;* after)
- **qabla** (*kab-lah;* before)
- **al-yawm** (*al-yah-oum;* today)
- **al-ghad** (*al-ghah-d;* tomorrow)
- **al-baariHa** (*al-bah-ree-hah;* yesterday)
- **ba'da al-ghad** (*bah-dah al-ghah-d;* the day after tomorrow)
- **qabla al-baariHa** (*kab-lah al-bah-ree-hah;* the day before yesterday)

Specifying the time of day

Because Arabic uses neither the a.m./p.m. system nor the 24-hour military clock when giving the time, you need to specify the time of day by actually saying what part of the day it is.

Here are the different times of day you're likely to use:

- **aS-SabaaH** (*ah-sah-bah;* morning, or sunrise to 11:59 a.m.)
- **aDH-DHuhr** (*ah-zoo-her;* noon, or 12:00 p.m.)
- **ba'da aDH-DHuhr** (*bah-dah ah-zoo-her;* afternoon, or 12:01 p.m. to 4:00 p.m.)
- **al-'asr** (*al-ah-ser;* late afternoon, or 4:01 p.m. to sunset)
- **al-masaa'** (*al-mah-sah;* evening, or sunset to two hours after sunset)
- **al-layl** (*ah-lah-yel;* night)

For example, if the time is 2:00 p.m., then you attach **ba'da aDH-DHuhr** to the proper ordinal. If sunset is at 6:00 p.m. and you want to say the time's 7:00 p.m., then you use **al-masaa'** and the ordinal because **al-masaa'** applies to the two-hour period right after sunset; if sunset is at 6:00 p.m. and you want to say the time's 9:00 p.m., then you use **al-layl** and the ordinal because 9:00 p.m. falls outside the scope of the evening convention.

The convention used to specify the part of the day is fairly straightforward:

> **as-saa'a** + ordinal number + **fii** (*fee;* in) + part of the day

The following are some examples to better illustrate responses to the question **kam as-saa'a?:**

- ✔ **as-saa'a al-waaHida fii ba'da aDH-DHuhr.** (*ah-sah-ah al-wah-hee-dah fee bah-dah ah-zoo-her;* It's 1:00 in the afternoon.)

- ✔ **as-saa'a al-khaamisa fii al-'asr.** (*ah-sah-ah al-kah-mee-sah fee al-ah-ser;* It's 5:00 in the late afternoon.)

- ✔ **as-saa'a al-Haadiya 'ashra fii aS-SabaaH.** (*ah-sah-ah al-hah-dee-yah ah-shrah fee ah-sah-bah;* It's 11:00 in the morning.)

- ✔ **as-saa'a at-taasi'a fii al-layl.** (*ah-sah-ah ah-tah-see-ah fee ah-lah-yel;* It's 9:00 in [at] night.)

- ✔ **as-saa'a as-saabi'a fii al-masaa'.** (*ah-sah-ah ah-sah-bee-ah fee al-mah-sah;* It's 7:00 in the evening.)

Specifying minutes

You can specify minutes in two different ways: noting the fractions of the hour, such as a half, a quarter, and a third, or actually spelling out the minutes.

When using the fraction method of telling minutes, use the following structure:

as-saa'a + ordinal number + **wa** (*wah;* and) + fraction

So what you're saying is "It's the second hour and a half," for example. In English transliteration, that's the equivalent of "It's half past two."

The main fractions you use are:

- ✔ **an-niSf** (*ah-nee-sef;* half)
- ✔ **ath-thuluth** (*ah-thoo-looth;* third)
- ✔ **ar-rubu'** (*ah-roo-booh;* quarter)
- ✔ **'ashara** (*ah-sha-rah;* tenth)

The following examples show you how to use the fraction method to specify minutes when telling time:

- ✔ **as-saa'a ath-thaaniya wa ar-rubu'.** (*ah-sah-ah ah-thah-nee-yah wah ah-roo-booh;* It's quarter past two.)
- ✔ **as-saa'a at-taasi'a wa an-niSf.** (*ah-sah-ah ah-tah-see-ah wah ah-nee-sef;* It's half past nine.)
- ✔ **as-saa'a al-khaamisa wa ar-rubu'.** (*ah-sah-ah al-kah-mee-sah wah ah-roo-booh;* It's quarter past five.)
- ✔ **as-saa'a al-Haadiya 'ashra wa an-niSf.** (*ah-sah-ah al-hah-dee-yah ah-shrah wah ah-nee-sef;* It's half past eleven.)

If you want to say "It's quarter of" or "It's twenty of", you need to use the preposition **'ilaa** (*ee-lah*), which means "of" or "to." If you think of the preposition **wa** as adding to the hour, then think of **'ilaa** as subtracting from the hour.

Because **'ilaa** subtracts from the hour, you must add one hour to whatever hour you're referring to. For example, if you want to say "It's 5:45," then you must say "It's quarter of six." Here are some examples that use **'ilaa:**

✔ **as-saa'a as-saadisa 'ilaa ar-rubu'.** (*ah-sah-ah ah-sah-dee-sah ee-lah ah-roo-booh;* It's quarter to six, or 5:45.)

✔ **as-saa'a al-waaHida 'ilaa ath-thuluth.** (*ah-sah-ah al-wah-hee-dah ee-lah ah-thoo-looth;* It's twenty to one, or 12:40.)

If you want to express minutes as a fraction and specify which time of day (a.m. or p.m.), you simply add **fii** and the time of day:

✔ **as-saa'a ath-thaamina wa ar-rubu' fii aS-SabaaH.** (*ah-sah-ah ah-thah-mee-nah wah ah-roo-booh fee ah-sah-bah;* It's 8:15 in the morning.)

✔ **as-saa'a al-khaamisa 'ilaa ar-rubu' fii al-'asr.** (*ah-sah-ah al-kah-mee-sah ee-lah ah-roo-booh fee al-ah-ser;* It's quarter to five in the late afternoon, or 4:45 p.m.)

You can also specify the minutes by actually spelling them out. Use the following format:

as-saa'a + ordinal/hours + **wa** + cardinal/minutes + **daqiiqa**

So **as-saa'a al-khaamisa wa 'khamsat daqiiqa** (*ah-sah-ah al-kah-mee-sah wah kam-sat dah-kee-qah*) means "It's 5:05." Here are some other examples:

✔ **as-saa'a al-waaHida wa 'ishriin daqiiqa.** (*ah-sah-ah al-wah-hee-dah wah eesh-reen dah-kee-qah;* It's 1:20.)

✔ **as-saa'a ath-thaamina wa khamsa wa 'arba'iin daqiiqa fii aS-SabaaH.** (*ah-sah-ah ah-thah-mee-nah wah kam-sah wah ar-bah-een dah-kee-qah;* It's 8:45 in the morning.)

Referring to Days and Months

The days of the **'usbuu'** (*ooh-seh-booh;* week) are derived from Arabic numbers. So recognizing the roots of the words for days of the week is key:

- **al-'aHad** (*al-ah-had;* Sunday)
- **al-'ithnayn** (*al-eeth-nah-yen;* Monday)
- **ath-thulathaa'** (*ah-thoo-lah-thah;* Tuesday)
- **al-'arbi'aa'** (*al-ah-reh-bee-ah;* Wednesday)
- **al-khamiis** (*al-khah-mees;* Thursday)
- **al-jumu'a** (*al-joo-moo-ah;* Friday)
- **as-sabt** (*ass-sah-bet;* Saturday)

al-jumu'a gets its name from **jumu'a,** which means "to gather;" it's the day when Muslims gather at the mosque and pray. Similarly, **as-sabt** is the day of rest, similar to the Jewish Sabbath.

Arabs use different types of calendars to note the passage of time, including these two:

- The **Gregorian calendar** is basically the same calendar as the one used throughout the Western world.
- The **Islamic calendar** is based on the lunar cycle and has different names for the months than its Western counterpart. It is based entirely on the moon's rotations and is used to identify specific religious holidays, such as the end and beginning of the holy month of Ramadan, in which Muslims fast from the break of dawn until dusk.

Tables 3-5 and 3-6 show the **ash-hur** (*ah-shuh-hur;* months) in the Gregorian and Islamic calendars.

Table 3-5	Gregorian Calendar	
Arabic	*Pronunciation*	*Translation*
Yanaayir	*yah-nah-yeer*	January
Fibraayir	*feeb-rah-yeer*	February
Maaris	*mah-rees*	March
'abriil	*ah-beh-reel*	April

Arabic	Pronunciation	Translation
Maayuu	*mah-yoo*	May
Yunyu	*yoo-neh-yoo*	June
Yulyu	*yoo-leh-yoo*	July
'aghusTus	*ah-goo-seh-toos*	August
Sibtambar	*seeb-tam-bar*	September
'uktuubar	*oo-key-too-bar*	October
Nufambar	*noo-fahm-bar*	November
Disambar	*dee-sahm-bar*	December

The Arabic names of the Gregorian months are similar to the names in English. However, the names of the Islamic calendar are quite different.

Table 3-6	Islamic Calendar
Arabic	**Pronunciation**
muHarram	*moo-hah-ram*
Safar	*sah-far*
rabii' al-awwal	*rah-bee al-ah-wall*
rabii' ath-thaanii	*rah-bee ah-thah-nee*
jumaada al-awwal	*joo-mah-dah al-ah-wall*
jumaada ath-thaanii	*joo-mah-dah ah-thah-nee*
rajab	*rah-jab*
sha'baan	*sha-huh-ban*
ramaDaan	*rah-mah-dan*
shawwaal	*shah-wuh-al*
dhuu al-qaa'ida	*zoo al-qah-ee-dah*
dhuu al-Hijja	*zoo al-hee-jah*

Because the Islamic calendar is based on the lunar cycle, the months don't overlap with the Gregorian calendar, making it difficult to match the months with the Gregorian ones.

To specify a date, such as December fifth, use the ordinal number. Because the terms for months are masculine, you must use masculine ordinals to identify specific dates. For example, you say **disambar al-khaamis** (*dee-sam-bar al-kah-mees;* December fifth) or **yanaayir aththaamin** (*yah-nah-yeer ah-thah-meen;* January eighth). In addition, because the ordinal acts as a possessive adjective, you must include the definite prefix **al-**.

Money, Money, Money

al-maal (*al-mal;* money) is an essential part of everyday life. Here are a few words to get you started:

- **fuluus** (*foo-loos;* cash/physical currency)
- **nuquud** (*noo-kood;* money/coins)
- **naqd** (*nah-ked;* coin)
- **'awraaq** (*aw-rak;* money/paper currencies)
- **biTaaqa al-'i'timaad** (*bee-tah-qah al-eeh-tee-mad;* credit card)
- **biTaaqaat al-'i'timaad** (*bee-tah-kat al-eeh-tee-mad;* credit cards)
- **biTaaqa al-'istilaaf** (*bee-tah-qah al-ees-tee-laf;* debit card)
- **shiik** (*sheek;* check)
- **shiikaat** (*shee-kat;* checks)
- **maSraf** (*mas-raf;* bank)
- **Hisaab maSrafii** (*hee-sab mas-rah-fee;* bank account)

Opening a bank account

One of the most important things you may do in a **maSraf** is open a **Hisaab maSrafii.** Here are two types of **Husub** (*hoo-soob;* accounts) you may inquire about:

> ✔ **Hisaab maSrafii 'aadii** (*hee-sab mas-rah-fee ah-dee;* checking account)

> ✔ **Hisaab maSrafii li at-tawfiir** (*hee-sab mas-rah-fee lee ah-taw-feer;* savings account)

You need to talk to the **'amiin al-maSraf** (*ah-meen al-mas-raf;* bank teller) (M) or the **'amiina al-masraf** (*ah-mee-nah al-mas-raf;* bank teller) (F) to open your **Hisaab:**

> ✔ **'uriidu 'an 'aftaHa Hisaab maSrafii.** (*oo-ree-doo an af-tah-hah hee-sab mas-rah-fee.* I would like to open a bank account.)

> ✔ **'ay 'anwaa' min al-Husub al-maSrafiiyya 'inda-kum?** (*ay an-wah meen al-hoo-soob al-mas-rah-fee-yah een-dah-koom?* What types of bank accounts do you have?)

> ✔ **maa huwa al-farq bayna al-Hisaab al-maSrafii al-'aadii wa al-Hisaab al-maSrafii li aT-Tulaab?** (*mah hoo-wah al-fah-rek bay-nah al-hee-sab al-mas-rah-fee al-ah-dee wah al-hee-sab al-mas-rah-fee lee ah-too-lab?* What's the difference between a regular checking account and a student checking account?)

Words to Know

yaftaHu	yaf-tah-hoo	to open
naw'	nah-weh	type
'anwaa'	an-wah	types
farq	fah-rek	difference
'arbuun	ar-boon	deposit
faa'ida	fah-ee-dah	interest rate
fii al-mi'a	fee al-mee-ah	percentage

The two basic transactions you'll probably make are:

- ✔ **wadii'a** (_wah-dee-ah;_ deposit)
- ✔ **'insiHaab** (_een-see-hab;_ withdrawal)

Using the ATM

Most ATMs accept all sorts of cards, whether they're issued by the same **maSraf** that operates the ATM terminal or not. However, some ATMs charge you a **'ujra** (_ooj-rah;_ fee) if you use a card not issued by a recognized **maSraf.** In addition, most ATMs accept both **biTaaqaat al-'i'timaad** (credit cards) and **biTaaqaat al-'istilaaf** (debit cards). *Note:* Another word for "credit card" is **biTaaqa diiniiya** (_bee-tah-qah dee-nee-yah_). Here are some ATM-related commands and phrases:

- ✔ **'udkhul al-biTaaqa** (_ood-kool al-bee-tah-qah;_ Insert the card.)
- ✔ **'udkhul ar-raqm as-siriiy.** (_ood-kool ah-rah-kem ah-see-ree;_ Enter the PIN/secret number.)
- ✔ **'insiHaab al-fuluus** (_een-see-hab al-foo-loos;_ cash withdrawal)
- ✔ **'udkhul al-kammiyya.** (_ood-kool al-kah-mee-yah;_ Enter the amount.)
- ✔ **'akkid al-kammiyya.** (_ah-keed al-kah-mee-yah;_ Confirm the amount.)
- ✔ **khudh al-fuluus.** (_kooz al-foo-loos;_ Take the cash.)
- ✔ **hal turiidu 'iiSaala?** (_hal too-ree-doo ee-sah-lah;_ Do you want a receipt?)
- ✔ **khudh al-'iiSaala.** (_kooz al-ee-sah-lah;_ Take the receipt.)
- ✔ **Haqqiq ar-raSiid.** (_hah-keek ah-rah-seed;_ Check the balance.)
- ✔ **Hawwil al-amwaal.** (_hah-weel al-am-wal;_ Transfer the money.)
- ✔ **'azil al-biTaaqa min faDlik.** (_ah-zeel al-bee-tah-qah meen fad-leek;_ Please remove the card.)

Exchanging currency

If you're traveling to a foreign **dawla** (*dah-ou-lah;* country), you won't get very far if you don't have the right **'umla mutadaawala** (*oom-lah moo-tah-dah-wah-lah;* currency), or **'umla** (*oom-lah*) for short. (Of course, you could rely on **shiikat al-musaafir** [*shee-kat al-moo-sah-feer;* traveler's checks], but you may find that carrying **'umla** is more convenient.) You can exchange **'umla** at a number of different places, at a **maSraf** or a **maktab as-sarf** (*mak-tab ah-sah-ref;* exchange desk).

The following list of questions can help you facilitate this exchange at the **maSraf**:

- ✔ **'ayna maktab as-sarf?** (*ay-nah mak-tab ah-sah-ref;* Where is the exchange desk?)

- ✔ **mataa yaHull maktab as-sarf?** (*mah-tah yah-hool mak-tab ah-sah-ref;* When does the exchange desk open?)

- ✔ **maa huwa mu'addal as-sarf al-yawm?** (*mah hoo-wah moo-ah-dal ah-sah-ref al-yah-oum;* What is today's exchange rate?)

- ✔ **hal mu'addal as-sarf sayakuun 'aHsan ghadan?** (*hal moo-ah-dal ah-sah-ref sah-yah-koon ah-san ghah-dan;* Will the exchange rate be better tomorrow?)

- ✔ **hal hunaaka 'ujra li tasriif al-fuluus?** (*hal hoo-nah-kah ooj-rah lee tas-reef al-foo-loos;* Is there a fee for exchanging money?)

- ✔ **'uriidu 'an 'aSrifa duularaat 'ilaa daraahim.** (*oo-ree-doo an as-ree-fah doo-lah-rat ee-lah dah-rah-heem;* I would like to exchange dollars into dirhams.)

- ✔ **kam min diinaar li mi'at duulaar?** (*kam meen dee-nar lee mee-at doo-lar;* How many dinars for 100 dollars?)

Here are some answers you may hear from the **'amiin maktab as-sarf** (*ah-meen mak-tab ah-sah-ref;* exchange desk representative):

✔ **na'am, nusarrif duulaaraat 'ilaa daraahim.**
(*nah-am, noo-sah-reef doo-lah-rat ee-lah dah-rah-heem;* Yes, we exchange dollars into dirhams.)

✔ **mu'addal as-sarf al-yawm mithla mu'addal as-sarf al-'ams.** (*moo-ah-dal ah-sah-ref al-yah-oum meet-lah moo-ah-dal ah-sah-ref al-ah-mes;* Today's exchange rate is the same as yesterday's exchange rate.)

✔ **naHnu naqbal duulaaraat faqat.** (*nah-noo nak-bal doo-lah-rat fah-kat;* We only accept dollars.)

✔ **naHnu naqbal nuquud faqat.** (*nah-noo nak-bal noo-kood fah-kat;* We only accept cash.)

✔ **mi'at duulaar tusaawii 'alf riyaal.** (*mee-at doo-lar too-sah-wee ah-lef ree-yal;* One hundred dollars equals one thousand riyals.)

✔ **hunaaka 'ujra 'ashrat duulaar li kul maHDar.** (*hoo-nah-kah ooj-ra ash-rat doo-lar lee kool mah-dar;* There is a ten dollar fee for every transaction.)

Chapter 4

Making New Friends and Enjoying Small Talk

· ·

In This Chapter

▶ Handling pleasantries

▶ Using common introductions

▶ Referring to countries and nationalities

▶ Asking questions

▶ Talking about yourself

· ·

1 n this chapter, I show you how to greet people in Arabic, how to respond to basic greetings, and how to interact with native Arabic speakers. You find out when it's appropriate to use formal and informal terms, how to make small talk, and how to introduce yourself. **HaDHan sa'iidan!** (*had-dan sa-ee-dan;* Good luck!)

Greetings!

In Arabic, the greeting you use depends on whom you're addressing. If you're greeting someone you don't know for the very first time, you must use the more formal greetings. If you're greeting an old family friend or a colleague you know well, feel free to use the more informal forms of greeting. If you're not sure which form to use, you're better off going formal.

You say hello . . .

The formal way of greeting someone in Arabic is '**as-salaamu 'alaykum** (*ass-sa-laam-ou a-lai-koum*). Even though it translates into English as "hello," it literally means "May peace be upon you."

Using '**as-salaamu 'alaykum** is appropriate when

> ✔ You're greeting a potential business partner.
>
> ✔ You're at a formal event, dinner, or gala.
>
> ✔ You're meeting someone for the first time.

The most common reply is **wa 'alaykum 'as-salaam** (*wa a-lai-koum ass-sa-laam;* and upon you peace).

The phrase '**ahlan wa sahlan** (*ahel-an wah sah-lan*) is a very informal way of greeting a person or group of people. Translated into English, it resembles the more informal "hi" as opposed to "hello." When someone says '**ahlan wa sahlan,** you should also reply '**ahlan wa sahlan.**

Using '**ahlan wa sahlan** is appropriate when

> ✔ You're greeting an old friend.
>
> ✔ You're greeting a family member.
>
> ✔ You're greeting someone at an informal gather-ing, such as a family lunch.

Simply saying '**ahlan!** is the most informal way of greeting someone. Use it only with people you're very comfortable with.

. . . I say goodbye

Saying goodbye in Arabic doesn't have formal or informal options. Here are the most common ways of saying goodbye in Arabic:

✔ **ma'a as-salaama** (*ma-a ass-sa-laa-ma;* go with peace, or goodbye)

✔ **'ilaa al-liqaa'** (*ee-laa al-li-kaa;* until next time)

✔ **'ilaa al-ghad** (*ee-laa al-gad;* see you tomorrow)

How are you doing?

The most common way to ask someone how he's doing is **kayf al-Haal?** (*ka-yef al-haal*), which literally means "How is the health?"

kayf al-Haal is gender-neutral, but you can also use gender-defined greeting terms, which are derivatives of the **kayf al-Haal** phrase:

✔ When addressing a man, use **kayf Haaluka** (*ka-yef haa-lou-ka*).

✔ When addressing a woman, use **kayf Haaluki** (*ka-yef haa-lou-kee*).

kayf Haalak? (*ka-yef haa-lak;* How is your health?) is a bit more personal and informal.

I'm doing well!

When someone asks you how you're doing, if you're doing just fine, the typical response is **al-Hamdu li-llah** (*al-ham-dou lee-lah*). It literally means "Praise to God," but in this context, it translates to "I'm doing well." Typically, after you say **al-Hamdu li-llah,** you follow up by saying **shukran** (*shouk-ran;* thank you).

After you say **al-Hamdu li-llah, shukran,** you need to ask the other person how he or she is doing:

✔ If you're speaking with a man, you say **wa 'anta kayf al-Haal** (*wa an-ta ka-yef al-haal;* And you, how are you?).

✔ If you're speaking with a woman, you say **wa 'anti kayf al-Haal** (*wa an-tee ka-yef al-haal;* And you, how are you?).

Making Introductions

This section explains how to ask people for their names and how to share your name using the possessive form.

Asking "What's your name?"

You need to know only two words: **'ism** (name) and **maa** (what). If you're addressing a man, you ask **maa 'ismuka?** (*maa ees-moo-ka;* What's your name?) (M). When addressing a woman, you ask **maa 'ismuki?** (*maa ees-moo-kee;* What's your name?) (F).

If you say **maa 'ismuk** without using the suffixes **–a** or **–i** at the end of **'ismuk,** you're actually using a gender-neutral form, which is perfectly acceptable. You can address both men and women by saying **maa 'ismuk?** (*maa ees-mook;* What's your name?) (GN).

Responding with "My name is . . ."

The possessive form is one of Arabic's easiest grammatical lessons: All you do is add the suffix **–ii** (pronounced *ee*) to the noun, and — voila! — you have the possessive form of the noun. To say "my name," add **–ii** to **'ism** and get **'ismii** (*ees-mee;* my name). So to say "My name is Amine," all you say is **'ismii amiin.**

When someone introduces himself or herself, a polite response is **tasharrafnaa** (*tah-shah-raf-nah;* It's a pleasure to meet you). You can also say **'ahlan wa sahlan** (*ahel-an wah sah-lan;* Nice to meet you.), which is much more informal.

Words to Know

'ahlan wa sahlan	ahel-an wa sah-lan	hi; or nice to meet you, depending on the context
al-Hamdu li-llah	al-ham-dou lee-lah	I'm doing well (Praise to God)
'ism	ee-ssam	name
'ismii	ees-mee	my name
masaa' al-khayr	ma-saa al-kha-yer	good evening
tasbaH 'alaa khayr	tas-bah 'a-la kha-yer	good night
'ilaa al-liqaa'	ee-laa al-li-qaa	until next time

Talking about Countries and Nationalities

When you meet someone for the first time, you may want to know what country he or she is from. Fortunately for English speakers, the Arabic names of many countries are similar to their names in English.

Asking "Where are you from?"

You can use these two phrases to ask someone where they're from:

✔ **min 'ayna 'anta** (*min ay-na ann-ta*) if you're asking a man.

✔ **min 'ayna 'anti** (*min ay-na ann-tee*) if you're asking a woman.

If you want to ask if a man is from a certain place — for example, America — you say

> **hal 'anta min 'amriikaa?** (*hal ann-ta min am-ree-kaa;* Are you from America?) (M)

If you're speaking with a woman, you simply replace **'anta** with **'anti.**

Answering "I am from . . ."

To say "I am from . . .," you use the preposition **min** (from) and the personal pronoun **'anaa** (I/me). Therefore, "I'm from America" is **'anaa min 'amriikaa.** It's that simple!

Table 4-1 lists the names of various countries and corresponding nationalities in Arabic.

Table 4-1   Country Names and Nationalities in Arabic

Country/Nationality	Pronunciation	Translation
al-maghrib	*al-magh-rib*	Morocco
maghribii	*magh-ree-bee*	Moroccan (M)
maghribiiyya	*magh-ree-bee-ya*	Moroccan (F)
al-jazaa'ir	*al-jah-zah-eer*	Algeria
jazaa'irii	*ja-zaa-ee-ree*	Algerian (M)
jazaa'iriiyya	*ja-zaa-ee-ree-ya*	Algerian (F)
tuunis	*tuu-nis*	Tunisia
tuunisii	*tuu-nee-see*	Tunisian (M)
tuunisiiyya	*tuu-nee-see-ya*	Tunisian (F)
miSr	*mee-sar*	Egypt
miSrii	*mees-ree*	Egyptian (M)
miSriiyya	*mees-ree-ya*	Egyptian (F)
al-'iraaq	*al-i-raa-q*	Iraq

Country/Nationality	Pronunciation	Translation
'iraaqii	ee-raa-qee	Iraqi (M)
'iraaqiiyya	ee-raa-qee-ya	Iraqi (F)
as-sa'uudiiyya	as-sa-uu-dee-ya	Saudi Arabia
sa'uudii	sa-uu-dee	Saudi (M)
sa'uudiiyya	sa-uu-dee-ya	Saudi (F)
'amriikaa	am-ree-kaa	America/USA
'amriikii	am-ree-kee	American (M)
'amriikiiyya	am-ree-kee-ya	American (F)

To tell someone "I am from Morocco," you say **'anaa min al-maghrib** (*ann-aa min al-magh-rib*). Alternatively, you may also say **'anaa maghribii** (*ann-aa magh-ree-bee;* I am Moroccan) (M).

Asking Questions

One of the best ways to start a conversation is to ask a **su'aal** (*soo-aahl;* question). To get you started, here are some key question words in Arabic:

- ✔ **man?** (*meh-n;* Who?)
- ✔ **'ayna?** (*eh-yeh-nah;* Where?)
- ✔ **mataa?** (*mah-taah;* When?)
- ✔ **maa?** (*maah;* What?)
- ✔ **maadhaa?** (*maah-zaah;* What?) (used with verbs)
- ✔ **lii maadhaa?** (*lee maah-zaah;* Why?)
- ✔ **kayfa?** (*keh-yeh-fah;* How?)
- ✔ **bikam?** (*bee-kah-m;* How much?)
- ✔ **kam min?** (*kam meen;* How many?)

You may use these question words to ask more elaborate and detailed questions. Here are some examples:

- **maa 'ismuka?** (*maah ees-moo-kah;* What's your name?) (MS)

- **maa 'ismuki?** (*maah ees-moo-kee;* What's your name?) (FS)

- **maa mihnatuka?** (*maah meeh-nah-too-kah;* What do you do?; literally "What is your job?") (MS)

- **maa mihnatuki?** (*maah meeh-nah-too-kee;* What do you do?; literally "What is your job?") (FS)

- **maadha taf'al?** (*maah-zaah tah-feh-al;* What are you doing?) (MS)

- **maadha taf'aliina?** (*maah-zaah tah-feh-alee-nah;* What are you doing?) (FS)

- **min 'ayna 'anta?** (*meh-n eh-yeh-nah ahn-tah;* Where are you from?) (MS)

- **min 'ayna 'anti?** (*meh-n eh-yeh-nah ahn-tee;* Where are you from?) (FS)

- **hal tuHibbu al-qiraa'a?** (*hal too-hee-buh al-kee-raa-ah;* Do you like to read?) (MS)

- **hal haadhaa kitaabuka?** (*hal hah-zah kee-tah-boo-kah;* Is this your book?)

- **'ayna maHaTTatu al-qiTaar?** (*eh-yeh-nah mah-hah-tah-too al-kee-taar;* Where is the train station?)

- **mataa satadhhab 'ilaa al-maTaar?** (*mah-taah sa-taz-hab ee-laah al-mah-taar;* When will she go to the airport?)

- **'ayna 'aHsan maT'am?** (*eh-yeh-nah ah-sah-n mah-tam;* Where is the best restaurant?)

Notice that some of the questions above refer to either masculine or feminine subjects. When you ask a question in Arabic, you choose the gender of the subject by modifying the gender suffix of the noun in question. For example, **kitaab** (*kee-tab*) means "book," but **kitaabuka** (*kee-tah-boo-kah*) means "your book" (M), and **kitaabuki** (*kee-tah-boo-kee*) means "your book" (F). So if you want to ask a man for his book, you use **kitaabuka**.

Talking about Yourself and Your Family

One of the best ways to get acquainted with someone is by finding out more about his or her **'usra** (*oos-rah;* family). Table 4-2 lists some important members of the **'usra** who may come up in conversation.

Table 4-2	All in the Family	
Arabic	*Pronunciation*	*Translation*
'ab	*ah-b*	father
'um	*oo-m*	mother
waalidayn	*wah-lee-day-en*	parents
'ibn	*ee-ben*	son
bint	*bee-net*	daughter
'abnaa'	*ah-ben-aah*	children
zawj	*zah-weh-j*	husband
zawja	*zah-weh-jah*	wife
'akh	*ah-kh-eh*	brother
'ukht	*oo-khe-t*	sister
jadd	*jah-d*	grandfather
jadda	*jah-dah*	grandmother
Hafiid	*hah-feed*	grandson
Hafiida	*hah-fee-dah*	granddaughter
'amm	*ahm*	paternal uncle (father's brother)
'amma	*ah-mah*	paternal aunt (father's sister)
khaal	*kah-l*	maternal uncle (mother's brother)
khaala	*kah-lah*	maternal aunt (mother's sister)

(continued)

Table 4-2 (continued)

Arabic	Pronunciation	Translation
zawj al-'amma	zah-weh-j al-ah-mah	paternal aunt's husband
zawjat al-'amm	zah-weh-jaht al-ahm	paternal uncle's wife
zawj al-khaala	zah-weh-j al-kah-lah	maternal aunt's husband
zawjat al-khaal	zah-weh-jaht al-kah-l	maternal uncle's wife
'ibn al-'amm	ee-ben al-ahm	male cousin from the father's side
bint al-'amm	bee-net al-ahm	female cousin from the father's side
'ibn al-khaal	ee-ben al-kah-l	male cousin from the mother's side
bint al-khaala	bee-net al-kah-lah	female cousin from the mother's side
'ahl az-zawj	ahel az-zah-weh-j	in-laws (M; collective)
'ahl az-zawja	ahel az-zah-weh-jah	in-laws (F; collective)
Hamou	hah-mooh	father-in-law
Hamaat	hah-maht	mother-in-law
silf	see-lef	brother-in-law
silfa	see-leh-fah	sister-in-law
rabboun	rah-boon	stepfather
rabba	rah-bah	stepmother
'akh min al-'ab	ah-kh-eh min al-ah-b	stepbrother from the father's side
'ukht min al-'ab	oo-khe-t min al-ah-b	stepsister from the father's side
'akh min al-'umm	ah-kh-eh min al-oo-m	stepbrother from the mother's side
'ukht min al-'umm	oo-khe-t min al-oo-m	stepsister from the mother's side

The **'usra** plays a very important role in Arab life, society, and culture, and the Arab **'usra** structure is very different than the Western family unit. The notion of the **'usra** is much more comprehensive and reinforced in the Arab world and the Middle East than it is in America or other Western countries. The family unit most prevalent in the West is the nuclear family — generally comprised of two parents and their children. But the **'usra** in the Arab world is an extended, close-knit family network made up of parents, children, grandparents, aunts, uncles, and cousins.

It's not uncommon to find an Arab household in which children live not only with their parents but also with their aunts, uncles, cousins, and grandparents. In Arab culture, the idea of the immediate family extends to second- and even third-degree cousins! In addition, lineage is important, and the terms for family relatives are specifically designed to differentiate between cousins from the mother's side (**'ibn al-khaal**) and cousins from the father's side (**'ibn al-'amm**). Thus, if you're talking to an Arab about his or her family, you can be sure that you'll have a lot to talk about!

Talking about Work

You can generally find out a lot about a person based on his or her **mihna** (_meeh-nah;_ job). If you want to ask someone about his or her profession, you have two options:

- ✔ **maa mihnatuka?** (_maah meeh-nah-too-kah;_ What is your job?; literally "What do you do?") (M)

- ✔ **maa mihnatuki?** (_maah meeh-nah-too-kee;_ What is your job?; literally "What do you do?") (F)

- ✔ **'ayna ta'mal?** (_eh-yeh-nah tah-mal;_ Where do you work?) (M)

- ✔ **'ayna ta'maliina?** (_eh-yeh-nah tah-mah-lee-nah;_ Where do you work?) (F)

Table 4-3 contains some important words relating to different occupations.

Table 4-3	Professions	
Arabic	*Pronunciation*	*Translation*
maSrafii	mah-srah-fee	banker (M)
SaHafii	sah-hah-fee	journalist (M)
kaatib	kah-teeb	writer (M)
mumathil	moo-mah-theel	actor (M)
muhandis	moo-han-dees	architect (M)
Tabiib	tah-beeb	doctor (M)
fannaan	fah-nan	artist (M)
mughannii	moo-ghah-nee	singer (M)
muTarjim	moo-tar-jeem	translator (M)
mumarriD	moo-mah-reed	nurse (M)
muHaamii	moo-hah-mee	lawyer (M)
Tabbaakh	tah-bah-kh	cook (M)
taajir	tah-jeer	merchant (M)
muHaasib	moo-hah-seeb	accountant (M)
simsaar	seem-sahr	broker (M)
Hallaaq	hah-lahk	barber (M)
fallaaH	fah-lah	farmer (M)
raaqiS	rah-kees	dancer (M)
shurTii	shoor-tee	police officer (M)
'iTfaa'ii	eet-fah-ee	fireman
rajul 'a'maal	rah-jool ah-maal	businessman

Table 4-3 gives the masculine forms of professions. To convert the masculine forms of professions into the feminine forms, simply add **fatHa.** For example, to say "translator" in the feminine, you add a **fatHa** to

muTarjim to get **muTarjima** (*moo-tar-jee-mah;* translator) (F). Take a look at the following conversation:

Alexandra: **maa mihnatuka?** (*maah meeh-nahtoo-kah?* What do you do?)

Hassan: **'anaa muhandis fii dar al-baydaa'.** (*ahnah moo-han-dees fee dar al-bay-dah.* I'm an architect in Casablanca.)

Alexandra: **haadhaa mumtaaz!** (*hah-zah moomtaz!* That's excellent!)

Hassan: **wa 'anti, 'ayna ta'maliina?** (*wah ahntee, eh-yeh-nah tah-mah-lee-nah?* And you, where do you work?)

Alexandra: **'anaa SaHafiyya.** (*ah-nah sah-hah-feeyah.* I'm a journalist.)

Hassan: **ma'a 'ayy jariida?** (*mah-ah ay jah-reedah?* With which newspaper?)

Alexandra: **ma'a nyuu yoork taymz.** (*mah-ah noo-york tie-mez.* With *The New York Times.*)

Shooting the Breeze: Talking about the Weather

If you want to engage in **kalaam khafiif,** shoot the breeze, or chitchat with a friend or stranger, talking about **Taqs** (*tah-kes;* weather) is a pretty safe topic. In conversations about **Taqs,** you're likely to use some of the following words:

- **shams** (*shah-mes;* sun)
- **maTar** (*mah-tar;* rain)
- **ra'd** (*rah-ed;* thunder)
- **barq** (*bah-rek;* lightning)
- **suHub** (*soo-hoob;* clouds)
- **Harara** (*hah-rah-rah;* temperature)
- **daraja** (*dah-rah-jah;* degrees)

- ✔ **bard** (*bah-red;* cold)

- ✔ **sukhoun** (*suh-koon;* hot)

- ✔ **ruTuuba** (*roo-too-bah;* humidity)

- ✔ **riiH** (*ree-eh;* wind)

- ✔ **'aaSifa** (*ah-tee-fah;* storm)

- ✔ **thalj** (*thah-lej;* snow)

- ✔ **qawsu quzaH** (*qah-wuh-suh koo-zah;* rainbow)

If you want to express the temperature, as in "It's x degrees," you must use the following construct: **al-Harara (insert number) daraja.** So, **al-Harara 35 daraja** means "It's 35 degrees."

Here are some expressions you can use to start talking about **Taqs:**

- ✔ **hal sayakun maTar al-yawm?** (*hal sah-yah-koon mah-tar al-yah-oum;* Is it going to rain today?)

- ✔ **yawm sukhoun, na'am?** (*yah-oum suh-koon, naham;* Hot day, isn't it?)

- ✔ **'inna yahubbu al-bard faj'atan.** (*ee-nah yah-hooboo al-bah-red fah-jeh-ah-tan;* It's gotten cold all of a sudden.)

- ✔ **kayfa aT-Taqs fii nyuu yoork?** (*keh-yeh-fah ah-tah-kes fii noo york?* How's the weather in New York?)

- ✔ **hal satakun shams?** (*hal sah-tah-koon shah-mes?* Is it going to be sunny?)

- ✔ **hal sayabqaa aT-Taqs haakadhaa kul al-usbuu'?** (*hal sah-yab-qah at-tah-kes hah-kah-zah kool al-oos-boo;* Will the weather remain like this all week?)

It would be difficult to chat about the weather without mentioning the **fuSuul** (*fuh-sool;* seasons):

- ✔ **Sayf** (*sah-yef;* summer)
- ✔ **khariif** (*kah-reef;* fall)
- ✔ **shitaa'** (*shee-tah;* winter)
- ✔ **rabii'** (*rah-beeh;* spring)

Temperatures in the majority of the Middle Eastern countries are stated in Celsius and not Fahrenheit. If you hear someone say that **al-harara 25 daraja** (*al-hah-rah-rah 25 dah-rah-jah;* It's 25 degrees), don't worry that you're going to freeze! They actually mean that it's almost 80 degrees Fahrenheit. To convert degrees from Celsius to Fahrenheit, use the following formula:

(Celsius x 1.8) + 32 = Degrees Fahrenheit

Chapter 5

Enjoying a Drink or a Snack (or a Meal!)

• •

In This Chapter

▶ Covering breakfast, lunch, and dinner

▶ Eating at home

▶ Dining at a restaurant

• •

Ta'aam (*tah-am;* food) is a great way to explore a new culture. In this chapter, you expand your vocabulary with the Arabic words for some popular meals and foods, and you find out how to place an order at a restaurant.

All about Meals

The three basic **wajbaat** (*waj-bat;* meals) in Arabic are:

> ✔ **fuTuur** (*foo-toor;* breakfast)
>
> ✔ **ghidaa'** (*gee-dah;* lunch)
>
> ✔ **'ishaa'** (*eeh-shah;* dinner)

Sometimes when you're feeling a little **jaai'** (*jah-eeh;* hungry) but aren't ready for a full course **wajba,** you may want a small **wajba khafiifa** (*waj-bah kah-fee-fah;* snack) instead.

Breakfast

fuTuur is the most important meal of the day. Here are some words that can help you start your morning right:

- **qahwa** (*qah-wah;* coffee)
- **kaHla** (*kah-lah;* black)
- **qahwa bi Haliib** (*qah-wah bee hah-leeb;* coffee with milk)
- **qahwa bi sukkar** (*qah-wah bee soo-kar;* coffee with sugar)
- **qahwa bi Haliib wa sukkar** (*qah-wah bee hah-leeb wah soo-kar;* coffee with milk and sugar)
- **shay** (*shay;* tea)
- **shay bi 'asal** (*shay bee ah-sel;* tea with honey)
- **khubz** (*koo-bez;* bread)
- **mu'ajjanaat** (*moo-ah-jah-nat;* pastries)
- **khubz muHammar** (*koo-bez moo-hah-mar;* toasted bread)
- **khubz bi zabda** (*koo-bez bee zab-dah;* bread with butter)
- **khubz bi zabda wa 'asal** (*koo-bez bee zab-dah wah ah-sal;* bread with butter and honey)
- **shefanj** (*sheh-fanj;* donuts)
- **Hubuub al-fuTuur** (*hoo-boob al-foo-toor;* breakfast cereal)
- **bayD** (*bah-yed;* eggs)
- **'aSiir** (*ah-seer;* juice)
- **'aSiir al-burtuqaal** (*ah-seer al-boor-too-kal;* orange juice)
- **'aSiir at-tuffaaH** (*ah-seer ah-too-fah;* apple juice)
- **'aSiir al-jazar** (*ah-seer al-jah-zar;* carrot juice)
- **Haliib** (*hah-leeb;* milk)

Do you typically grab your breakfast on the go? Here are some phrases to help you out:

Laura: **SabaaH al-khayr 'aHmad.** (*sah-bah al-kah-yer ah-mad.* Good morning Ahmed.)

Ahmed: **SabaaH an-nuur lora. maadhaa tuHib-biina haadha aS-SabaaH?** (*sah-bah ah-noor loh-rah. mah-zah too-hee-bee-nah hah-zah ah-sah-bah?* Good morning Laura. What would you like this morning?)

Laura: **al-'aadii.** (*al-ah-dee.* The usual.)

Ahmed: **fawran. qahwa wa Haliib, na'am?** (*faw-ran. qah-wah wah hah-leeb, nah-am?* Right away. Coffee with milk, right?)

Laura: **na'am.** (*nah-am.* Yes.)

Ahmed: **kam min mil'aqat as-sukkar?** (*kam meen meel-ah-kat ah-soo-kar?* How many spoons of sugar?)

Laura: **mil'aqatayn.** (*meel-ah-qah-tayn.* Two spoons.)

Ahmed: **hal tuHibbiina al-qahwa Saghiira 'aadiya 'aw kabiira?** (*hal too-hee-bee-nah al-qah-wah sah-ghee-rah ah-dee-yah aw kah-bee-rah?* Would you like a small, medium, or large coffee?)

Laura: **'uHibbu qahwa kabiira al-yawm.** (*oo-hee-boo qah-wah kah-bee-rah al-yah-oum.* I'd like a large coffee today.)

Ahmed: **wa hal turiidiina shay'un li al-'akl?** (*wah hal too-ree-dee-nah shay-oon lee al-ah-kel?* And would you like anything to eat?)

Laura: **hal 'indaka shefanj?** (*hal een-dah-kah sheh-fanj?* Do you have donuts?)

Ahmed: **na'am. kam min shefanja turiidiina?** (*nah-am. kam meen sheh-fan-jah too-ree-dee-nah?* Yes. How many donuts do you want?)

Laura: **'uriidu thalaathat shefanja min faDlik.** (*oo-ree-doo thah-lah-that sheh-fan-jah meen fad-leek.* I'd like three donuts please.)

A piece of **faakiha** (*fah-kee-hah;* fruit) is a healthy addition to any **fuTuur.** Here are some common **fawaakih** (*fah-wah-keeh;* fruits):

- **burtuqaala** (*boor-too-kal-ah;* orange)
- **tufaaHa** (*too-fah-hah;* apple)
- **mawza** (*maw-zah;* banana)
- **tuuta** (*too-tah;* strawberry)
- **'ijaaS** (*ee-jas;* pear)
- **dallaaHa** (*dah-lah-hah;* watermelon)
- **baTTiikh** (*bah-teek;* cantaloupe)
- **khawkha** (*kaw-kah;* peach)
- **'inab** (*ee-nab;* grapes)
- **laymoon** (*lay-moon;* lemon)
- **laymoon hindii** (*lay-moon heen-dee;* grapefruit)
- **laymoon maaliH** (*lay-moon mah-leeh;* lime)
- **al-anbaj** (*al-ann-baj;* mango)

Lunch

Eating your **fuTuur** keeps you **shab'aan** (*shab-an;* satisfied) for a few hours. When you get **jaai'** (*jah-eeh;* hungry) again, it's time for **al-ghidaa'** (*al-gee-dah;* lunch).

al-ghidaa' is a very important **wajba** (*waj-bah;* meal). In most Middle Eastern countries, workers don't sit in their cubicles and eat their **ghidaa'.** Rather, most offices close and employees get two hours or more for **al-ghidaa'!**

Here are some of the common **Ta'aam** (*tah-am;* foods) you can expect during the **ghidaa':**

- **laHam** (*lah-ham;* meat)
- **laHam al-baqar** (*lah-ham al-bah-kar;* beef)
- **laHam al-ghanam** (*lah-ham al-ghah-nam;* lamb)
- **laHam al-'ajal** (*lah-ham al-ah-jel;* veal)

- ✔ **samak** (*sah-mak;* fish)
- ✔ **dajaaj** (*dah-jaj;* chicken)
- ✔ **ruz** (*rooz;* rice)

Sometimes, your **ghidaa'** may consist of a simple **sand-wiish** (*sand-weesh;* sandwich). Other times, you may prefer a nice, healthy **salada** (*sah-lah-dah;* salad). Here are some **khudar** (*koo-dar;* vegetables) to help you make your **salada ladhiidha** (*lah-zee-zah;* delicious):

- ✔ **khass** (*kass;* lettuce)
- ✔ **TamaaTim** (*tah-mah-teem;* tomatoes)
- ✔ **khurshuuf** (*koor-shoof;* artichokes)
- ✔ **baTaaTis** (*bah-tah-tees;* potatoes)
- ✔ **hilyoon** (*heel-yoon;* asparagus)
- ✔ **'afookaat** (*ah-foo-kat;* avocado)
- ✔ **qarnabiiT** (*kar-nah-beet;* broccoli)
- ✔ **qunnabiiT** (*koo-nah-beet;* cauliflower)
- ✔ **dhurra** (*zoo-rah;* corn)
- ✔ **khiyaar** (*kee-yar;* cucumber)
- ✔ **fuul** (*fool;* beans)
- ✔ **'ayshu al-ghuraab** (*ay-shoo al-ghoo-rab;* mushrooms)
- ✔ **baSla** (*bass-lah;* onions)
- ✔ **baziilya** (*bah-zee-lee-yah;* peas)
- ✔ **'isfaanaakh** (*ees-fah-nak;* spinach)

In order to make a **sandwiish** even more delicious, add some of the following **Tawaabil** (*tah-wah-beel;* condiments):

- ✔ **SalSa min aT-TamaaTim** (*sal-sah meen at-tah-mah-teem;* ketchup)
- ✔ **khardal** (*kar-dal;* mustard)
- ✔ **miiyooniiz** (*mee-yoo-neez;* mayonnaise)
- ✔ **mukhallalaat** (*moo-kah-lah-lat;* pickles)

If you're particular about how you like your sandwich, the following phrases will help you out when you head to the sandwich shop:

Nawal: **'ahlan. kayfa yumkin 'an 'usaa'iduka?** (*ahel-an. kay-fah yoom-keen an oo-sah-ee-doo-kah?* Hi. How may I help you?)

Matt: **'uriidu 'an 'aTlub sandwiish min faDlik.** (*oo-ree-doo an at-loob sand-weesh meen fad-leek.* I would like to order a sandwich please.)

Nawal: **'ay Hajem sandwiish turiid: kabiir 'aw Saghiir?** (*ay hah-jem sand-weesh too-reed: kah-beer aw sah-gheer?* What size sandwich do you want: large or small?)

Matt: **as-sandwiish al-kabiir.** (*ah-sand-weesh al-kah-beer.* The large sandwich.)

Nawal: **'ay naw' min khubz tuHibb: khubz 'abyaD 'aw khubz az-zara'?** (*ay nah-ouh meen koo-bez too-heeb: koo-bez ab-yad aw koo-bez ah-zah-rah?* What type of bread would you like: white bread or whole wheat bread?)

Matt: **khubz 'abyaD.** (*koo-bez ab-yad.* White bread.)

Nawal: **'indanaa jamii' al-alHaam: laHam al-ghanam, laHam al-baqar wa laHam al-'ajal. wa 'indanaa dajaaj 'ayDan. 'ay laHam turiid fii as-sandwiish?** (*een-dah-nah jah-meeh al-al-ham: lah-ham al-ghah-nam, lah-ham al-bah-kar wah lah-ham al-ah-jal. wah een-dah-nah dah-jaj ay-zan. ay lah-ham too-reed fee ah-sand-weesh?* We have all sorts of meat: lamb, beef, and veal. And we also have chicken. What kind of meat do you want in the sandwich?)

Matt: **dajaaj min faDlik.** (*dah-jaj meen fad-leek.* Chicken please.)

Nawal: **wa hal tuHibb khudar fii as-sandwiish?** (*wah hal too-heeb koo-dar fee ah-sand-weesh?* And would you like any vegetables in your sandwich?)

Matt: **na'am. hal 'indakum TamaaTim?** (*nah-am. hal een-dah-koom tah-mah-teem?* Yes. Do you have any tomatoes?)

Nawal: **na'am. shay' 'aakhar?** (*nah-am. shay ah-kar?* Yes. Anything else?)

Matt: **khass, qarnabiiT wa baSla.** (*kass, kar-nah-beet wah bas-lah.* Lettuce, broccoli, and onions.)

Nawal: **'afwan, ma 'indanaa qarnabiiT.** (*af-wan, mah een-dah-nah kar-nah-beet.* I apologize, we don't have any broccoli.)

Matt: **Tayyib. Khass wa TamaaTim faqat.** (*tah-yeeb. kass, wah tah-mah-teem fah-kat.* That's okay. Lettuce and tomatoes will do.)

Nawal: **wa hal turiid Tawaabil?** (*wah hal too-reed tah-wah-beel?* And do you want condiments?)

Matt: **mukhallalaat faqat. shukran.** (*moo-kah-lah-lat fah-kat. shook-ran.* Pickles only. Thank you.)

Words to Know

'aTlub	at-loob	order
Hajem	hah-jem	size
naw'	nah-ouh	type
khubz 'abyaD	koo-bez ab-yad	white bread
khubz az-zara'	koo-bez ah-zah-rah	whole wheat bread
jamii'	jah-meeh	all sorts
faqat	fah-kat	only

The most important **fi'l** (*fee-al;* verb) you should know relating to **Ta'aam** is the verb **'akala** (*ah-kah-lah*), which means "ate" in the past tense. In the present tense, it's conjugated as **ya'kulu** (*yah-koo-loo;* to eat). See Tables 5-1 and 5-2.

Table 5-1   The Past Tense of the Verb *'akala* (To Eat)

Form	Pronunciation	Translation
'anaa 'akaltu	*ah-nah ah-kal-too*	I ate
'anta 'akalta	*ahn-tah ah-kal-tah*	You ate (MS)
'anti 'akalti	*ahn-tee ah-kal-tee*	You ate (FS)
huwa 'akala	*hoo-wah ah-kah-lah*	He ate
hiya 'akalat	*hee-yah ah-kah-lat*	She ate
naHnu 'akalnaa	*nah-noo ah-kal-nah*	We ate
'antum 'akaltum	*ahn-toom ah-kal-toom*	You ate (MP)
'antunna 'akaltunna	*ahn-too-nah ah-kal-too-nah*	You ate (FP)
hum 'akaluu	*hoom ah-kah-loo*	They ate (MP)
hunna 'akalna	*hoo-nah ah-kal-nah*	They ate (FP)
antumaa 'akaltumaa	*ahn-too-mah ah-kal-too-mah*	You ate (dual/MP/FP)
humaa 'akalaa	*hoo-mah ah-kah-lah*	They ate (dual/MP)
humaa 'akalataa	*hoo-mah ah-kah-lah-tah*	They ate (dual/FP)

Table 5-2	Present Tense Conjugation of *ya'kulu* (To Eat)	
Form	**Pronunciation**	**Translation**
'anaa 'a'kulu	*ah-nah ah-koo-loo*	I am eating
'anta ta'kulu	*ahn-tah tah-koo-loo*	You are eating (MS)
'anti ta'kuliina	*ahn-tee tah-koo-lee-nah*	You are eating (FS)
huwa ya'kulu	*hoo-wah yah-koo-loo*	He is eating
hiya ta'kulu	*hee-yah tah-koo-loo*	She is eating
naHnu na'kulu	*nah-noo nah-koo-loo*	We are eating
'antum ta'kuluuna	*ahn-toom tah-koo-loo-nah*	You are eating (MP)
'antunna ta'kulna	*ahn-too-nah tah-kool-nah*	You are eating (FP)
hum ya'kuluuna	*hoom yah-koo-loo-nah*	They are eating (MP)
hunna ya'kulna	*hoo-nah yah-kool-nah*	They are eating (FP)
antumaa ta'kulaani	*ahn-too-mah tah-koo-lah-nee*	You are eating (dual/MP/FP)
humaa ya'kulaani	*hoo-mah yah-koo-lah-nee*	They are eating (dual/MP)
humaa ta'kulaani	*hoo-mah tah-koo-lah-nee*	They are eating (dual/FP)

Dinner

In most Arab countries, **'ishaa'** (*eeh-shah;* dinner) is usually eaten very late, around 9 or even 10 p.m. Because **ghidaa'** and **fuTuur** are the meals at which people eat a lot, and because of the traditionally late hour of **'ishaa',** most people in the Arab world have light meals during **'ishaa'.**

A typical **'ishaa'** consists of some sort of **samak** (*sah-mak;* fish), **dajaaj** (*dah-jaj;* chicken), or other kind of **laHm** (*lah-hem;* meat).

Enjoying a Meal at Home

This section covers key terms to help you prepare and set the table for a **wajba ladhiida fii al-manzil** (*waj-bah lah-zee-zah fee al-man-zeel;* a delicious home-cooked meal)!

Here are some common items you might find in your **maTbakh** (*mat-bak;* kitchen):

- ✔ **furn** (*foo-ren;* stove)
- ✔ **thallaaja** (*thah-lah-jah;* refrigerator)
- ✔ **maghsala** (*mag-sah-lah;* sink)
- ✔ **khizaanaat** (*kee-zah-nat;* cupboards)
- ✔ **milH** (*mee-leh;* salt)
- ✔ **fulful** (*fool-fool;* pepper)
- ✔ **zayt az-zaytuun** (*zah-yet ah-zay-toon;* olive oil)

When you're done **Tibaakha** (*tee-bah-kah;* cooking) **daakhil** (*dah-keel;* inside) the **maTbakh,** you're ready to step into the **ghurfat al-'akel** (*ghoor-fat al-ah-kel;* dining room) and set up the **Ta'aam** on top of the **maa'ida** (*mah-ee-dah;* dining table). Here are some items you may find on your **maa'ida:**

- ✔ **'aS-SHaan** (*ass-han;* plates)
- ✔ **'aTbaaq** (*at-bak;* dishes)
- ✔ **ku'uus** (*koo-oos;* glasses)
- ✔ **'akwaab** (*ak-wab;* tumblers)
- ✔ **'awaan fiDDiyya** (*ah-wan fee-dee-yah;* silverware)
- ✔ **shawkaat** (*shaw-kat;* forks)

✔ **malaa'iq** (*mah-lah-eek;* spoons)

✔ **sakaakiin** (*sah-kah-keen;* knives)

✔ **manaadil** (*mah-nah-deel;* napkins)

Dining Out

Going to a nice **maT'am** (*mat-am;* restaurant) is one of my favorite things to do. In this section, you find out how to interact with the wait staff and choose the best food.

The dining experience in most restaurants in the Middle East, as well as in Middle Eastern restaurants all over the world, is truly an enchanting and magical experience. The décor is usually very ornate and sumptuous, with oriental patterns and vivid colors adorning the rooms. The wait staff usually wears traditional **jellaba** (*jeh-lah-bah*), which are long, flowing garments that are pleasing to the eye, and the food is very exotic, spicy, and delicious. When you go to a Middle Eastern restaurant, allow at least a couple of hours for the dining experience — don't be surprised if you end up savoring a five- or even seven-course meal!

Perusing the menu

As in other restaurants, the **qaa'imat aT-Ta'aam** (*qah-ee-mah ah-tah-am;* menu) in Middle Eastern restaurants is usually divided into three sections:

✔ **muqabbilaat** (*moo-qah-bee-lat;* appetizers)

✔ **Ta'aam ra'iisii** (*tah-am rah-ee-see;* main course/ entrees)

✔ **taHliya** (*tah-lee-yah;* dessert)

Appetizers

In the **muqabbilaat** section of the menu, you find some **Ta'aam khafiif** (*tah-am kah-feef;* light food) to help build your appetite. Here are some common **muqabbilaat:**

- **rubyaan** (*roob-yan;* shrimp)

- **baadhinjaan** (*bah-zeen-jan;* eggplant)

- **kam'a** (*kam-ah;* truffles)

- **thuum muHammar** (*toom moo-hah-mar;* roasted garlic)

- **waraq 'ay-nab** (*wah-rak ay-nab;* stuffed grape leaves)

- **'adas** (*ah-das;* lentils)

- **Hasaa'** (*hah-sah;* soup)

- **Hariira** (*hah-ree-rah;* Moroccan soup)

Entrees

The **Ta'aam ra'iisii** consist of dishes featuring **dajaaj** (*dah-jaj;* chicken), various other **laHam** (*lah-ham;* meat), and **samak** (*sah-mak;* fish). Most restaurants have a pretty extensive selection of **samak,** including:

- **salmoon** (*sal-moon;* salmon)

- **al-qood** (*al-kood;* cod)

- **tuun** (*toon;* tuna)

- **al-'uTruuT** (*al-oot-root;* trout)

- **'isqoomrii** (*ees-koom-ree;* mackerel)

- **shabbooT** (*shah-boot;* carp)

- **moosaa** (*moo-sah;* sole)

- **qirsh** (*kee-resh;* shark)

Desserts

The **taHliya** is a great way to wrap up a nice **wajba.** I like the **taHliya** because there are a lot of

Halawiyyaat (*hah-lah-wee-yat;* sweets) to choose from. Here are some popular **taHliya:**

- ✔ **ka'k** (*kahk;* cake)
- ✔ **ka'k ash-shuukuulaat** (*kahk ah-shoo-koo-lat;* chocolate cake)
- ✔ **Buudha** (*boo-zah;* ice cream)
- ✔ **'aTbaaq** (*at-bak;* pudding)
- ✔ **al-jubun** (*al-joo-boon;* cheese)

Beverages

In addition to **Ta'aam,** you may also notice a portion of the menu — or an entirely different menu — introducing different kinds of **mashruubaat** (*mash-roo-bat;* drinks). The following are some **mashruubaat** you may come across in the **qaa'imat aT-Ta'aam:**

- ✔ **maa'** (*mah;* water)
- ✔ **maa' ghaaziya** (*mah ghah-zee-yah;* soda water)
- ✔ **'aSiir al-laymoon** (*ah-seer ah-lay-moon;* lemonade)
- ✔ **al-khamer** (*al-kah-mer;* alcohol)
- ✔ **biirra** (*bee-rah;* beer)
- ✔ **nabiidh** (*nah-beez;* wine)
- ✔ **nabiidh 'aHmar** (*nah-beez ah-mar;* red wine)
- ✔ **nabiidh 'abyaD** (*nah-beez ab-yad;* white wine)

Placing your order

After you peruse the **qaa'imat aT-Ta'aam,** you're ready to place your order with either the

- ✔ **khaadim al-maT'am** (*kah-deem al-mat-am;* waiter) or the
- ✔ **khaadimat al-maT'am** (*kah-dee-maht al-mat-am;* waitress).

maT'am staff are usually highly trained individuals who know the ins and outs of the **Ta'aam** that the **maT'am** serves, so don't be afraid to ask lots of **'as'ila** (*ass-ee-lah;* questions) about things on the **qaa'imat aT-Ta'aam.** Here's how you might order:

Waitress: **marHaba bikum 'ilaa maT'am 'aTlas. kayfa yumkin 'an 'usaa'idukum?** (*mar-hah-bah bee-koom ee-lah mat-ham at-las. kay-fah yoom-keen an oo-sah-ee-doo-koom?* Welcome to Restaurant Atlas. How may I help you?)

Sam: **'ay mashruubaat 'indakum?** (*ay mash-roo-bat een-dah-koom?* What do you have to drink?)

Waitress: **'indanaa maa', maa' ghaaziya wa 'aSiir al-laymoon.** (*een-dah-nah mah, mah ghah-zee-yah wah ah-seer ah-lay-moon.* We have water, soda water, and lemonade.)

Sam: **sa-nabda' bi maa' min faDlik.** (*sah-nab-dah bee mah meen fad-leek.* We'll start with water please.)

Waitress: **turiidaani maa' Tabi'ii 'aw maa' 'aadii?** (*too-ree-dah-nee mah tah-bee-eey aw mah ah-dee?* Do you want mineral [bottled] water or regular [tap] water?)

Sam: **maa' Tabi'ii.** (*mah tah-bee-eey.* Mineral water.)

Waitress: **fawran. hal turiidaani khamer 'ayDan?** (*faw-ran. hal too-ree-dah-nee kah-mer ay-zan?* Right away. And would you like any alcoholic drinks as well?)

Atika: **hal 'indakum nabiidh?** (*hal een-dah-koom nah-beez?* Do you have any wine?)

Waitress: **na'am. 'indanaa nabiidh 'abyaD wa nabiidh 'aHmar.** (*nah-am. een-dah-nah nah-beez ab-yad wah nah-beez ah-mar.* Yes. We have white wine and red wine.)

Atika: **sa-na'khudh nabiidh 'aHmar min faDlik.** (*sah-nah-kooz nah-beez ah-mar meen fad-leek.* We'll have red wine please.)

Waitress: **mumtaaz. sa 'a'Tiikum waqt li-taqra'aani al-qaa'ima.** (*moom-taz. sah ah-tee-koom wah-ket lee-tak-rah-ah-nee al-qah-ee-mah.* Excellent. I'll give you some time to read through the menu.)

Sam: **shukran.** (*shook-ran.* Thank you.)

Waitress: **hal 'antumaa musta'idaani li-'iTlaab aT-Ta'aam?** (*hal an-too-mah moos-tah-ee-dah-nee lee-eet-lab ah-tah-am?* Are you ready to place your order?)

Atika: **na'am. li al-muqabbilaat sa-nabda' bi rubyaan wa kam'a.** (*nah-am. lee al-moo-qah-bee-lat sah-nab-dah bee roob-yan wah kam-ah.* Yes. For appetizers, we'd like shrimp and truffles.)

Waitress: **'ikhtiyaar mumtaaz.** (*eek-tee-yar moom-taz.* Excellent selection.)

Sam: **wa ba'da dhaalika sa-na'khudh salmoon.** (*wah bah-dah zah-lee-kah sa-nah-kooz sal-moon.* And after that we'd like to have salmon.)

Waitress: **shay' 'aakhar?** (*shay ah-kar?* Anything else?)

Atika: **nuriid ka'k ash-shuukuulaat li at-taHliya.** (*noo-reed kahk ah-shoo-koo-lat lee ah-tah-lee-yah.* We'd like the chocolate cake for dessert.)

Finishing your meal and paying the bill

When you finish your meal, you need to take care of your **Hisaab** (*hee-sab;* bill). You may ask your waiter for the bill by saying **al-Hisaab min faDlik** (*al-hee-sab meen fad-leek;* the bill please). Another option is to ask the waiter or waitress **kam al-kaamil?** (*kam al-kah-meel;* What's the total?).

Like in the United States, tipping your waiter or waitress is customary in Arabic-speaking countries and Middle Eastern restaurants. The amount of the **baqsheeh** (*bak-sheesh;* tip) depends on the kind of service you received, but usually 15 to 20 percent is average.

Chapter 6

Shop 'til You Drop!

- -

In This Chapter

▶ Browsing inside the store

▶ Comparing items and costs

▶ Identifying clothing sizes and colors

- -

*W*hether you're hardcore or just window shopping, this chapter gives you what you need to know.

Going to the Store

When you want to buy something, you head to the **dukkaan** (*doo-kan;* store). Depending on your shopping list, you can choose from different types of **dakaakiin** (*dah-kah-keen;* stores). Here are some specialty **dakaakiin** you may need to visit:

- **makhbaza** (*mak-bah-zah;* bakery)
- **maktaba** (*mak-tah-bah;* bookstore/library)
- **dukkaan al-malaabis** (*doo-kan al-mah-lah-bees;* clothing store)
- **dukkaan al-iliktroniyaat** (*doo-kan al-ee-leek-troo-nee-yat;* electronics store)
- **dukkaan al-Halawiyyaat** (*doo-kan al-hah-lah-wee-yat;* pastry shop)
- **dukkaan al-baqqaal** (*doo-kan al-bah-kal;* grocery store)

- ✔ **dukkaan as-samak** (*doo-kan ah-sah-mak;* fish store)

- ✔ **jawharii** (*jaw-hah-ree;* jeweler)

Other types of **dakaakiin** provide services, such as haircuts and manicures. Here are some **dakaakiin** that are more service-oriented:

- ✔ **maktab as-siyaaHa** (*mak-tab ah-see-yah-hah;* travel agency)

- ✔ **Hallaaq** (*hah-lak;* barber/hairdresser)

- ✔ **dukkaan al-jamal** (*doo-kan al-jah-mal;* beauty parlor)

If you need to shop for a variety of goods, your destination is the **dukkaan kabiir** (*doo-kan kah-beer;* department store/mall), where you can find almost anything you want.

Browsing the merchandise

Sometimes you just need to browse. If so, a **khaadim ad-dukkaan** (*kah-deem ah-doo-kan;* store clerk) (M) or a **khaadima ad-dukkaan** (*kah-dee-mah ah-doo-kan;* store clerk) (F) may ask:

- ✔ **hal yumkin 'an 'usaa'iduka?** (*hal yoom-keen an oo-sah-ee-doo-kah?;* May I help you?) (M)

- ✔ **hal yumkin 'an 'usaa'iduki?** (*hal yoom-keen an oo-sah-ee-doo-kee?;* May I help you?) (F)

- ✔ **hal turiidu shay' khaaS?** (*hal too-ree-doo shay kas?;* Are you looking for anything in particular?) (M)

- ✔ **hal turiidiina shay' khaaS?** (*hal too-ree-dee-nah shay kas?;* Are you looking for anything in particular?) (F)

If you need **musaa'ada** (*moo-sah-ah-dah;* help/assistance), simply respond by saying **na'am** (*nah-am;* yes). Otherwise, if you want to continue browsing, **laa**

shukran (*lah shook-ran;* no thank you) should do the trick.

Getting around the store

If you want **tawjiihaat** (*taw-jee-hat;* directions) to part of the store, head to the **maktab al-'i'laamaat** (*mak-tab al-eeh-lah-mat;* information desk) to have your **'as'ila** (*ass-ee-lah;* questions) answered. Here are some **'as'ila** to help you practice:

- ✔ **hal yumkin 'an tusaa'idunii?** (*hal yoom-keen an too-sah-ee-doo-nee;* Is it possible for you to help me?)

- ✔ **'ayna aT-Tabiq al-'awwal?** (*ay-nah ah-tah-beek al-ah-wal;* Where is the first floor?)

- ✔ **'ayna al-miS'ad?** (*ay-nah al-mees-ad;* Where is the elevator?)

- ✔ **hal hunaaka miS'ad 'ilaa aT-Tabaq al-khaamis?** (*hal hoo-nah-kah mees-ad ee-lah ah-tah-bak al-kah-mees?* Is there an elevator to the fifth floor?)

- ✔ **'ayna maHall al-malaabis?** (*ay-nah mah-hal al-mah-lah-bees;* Where is the section for clothes?)

- ✔ **fii 'ay Tabaq al-jawharii?** (*fee ay tah-baq al-jaw-hah-ree;* On which floor is the jeweler located?)

- ✔ **hal hunaaka makhbaza fii ad-dukaan al-kabiir?** (*hal hoo-nah-kah mak-bah-zah fee ah-doo-kan al-kah-beer;* Is there a bakery in the mall?)

Words to Know

yabHathu	yab-hah-thoo	searching
maHall	mah-hal	section
nisaa'	nee-sah	women

continued

Words to Know *(continued)*

rijaal	ree-jal	men
banaat	bah-nat	girls
'awlaad	aw-lad	boys
Tabiq	tah-beek	floor
miS'ad	mees-ad	elevator
yamiin	yah-meen	right
yaSaar	yah-sar	left
yamiinuki	yah-mee-noo-kee	your right (F)
yamiinuka	yah-mee-noo-kah	your right (M)
yaSaaruki	yah-sah-roo-kee	your left (F)
yaSaaruka	yah-sah-roo-kah	your left (M)
daakhil	dah-keel	inside
khaarij	kah-reej	outside

Asking for a Particular Item

When you want a particular item, you're likely to need
a demonstrative word, such as "that one" or "this" or
"those over there." *Demonstratives* are the little words
we use to specify particular items. Table 6-1 presents
the common demonstratives in Arabic:

Table 6-1	Arabic Demonstratives	
Arabic	*Pronunciation*	*Translation*
haadhaa	*hah-zah*	this (MS)
haadhihi	*hah-zee-hee*	this (FS)
dhaalika	*zah-lee-kah*	that (MS)
Tilka	*teel-kah*	that (FS)
haa'ulaa'ii	*hah-oo-lah-ee*	these (gender neutral)
'ulaa'ika	*oo-lah-ee-kah*	those (gender neutral)

In a sentence, you always place the demonstrative word *before* the object being pointed to, which is often a noun. In addition, the noun must be defined using the definite prefix pronoun **al-**.

The following conversation illustrates some common demonstratives:

Omar: **hal 'indakum jakiiTaat?** (*hal een-dah-koom jah-kee-tat?* Do you have jackets?)

Salesperson: **na'am. 'indanaa 'anwaa' kathiira min aj-jakiiTaat. 'an 'ay naw' tabHathu?** (*nah-am. een-dah-nah an-wah kah-thee-rah meen ah-jah-kee-tat. an ay nah-weh tab-hah-thoo?* Yes. We have many different kinds of jackets. Which kind are you looking for?)

Omar: **'uriidu jakiiTa bi aj-jald.** (*oo-ree-doo jah-kee-tah bee ah-jah-led.* I want a leather jacket.)

Salesperson: **Tayyib. 'itba'nii min faDlik.** (*tah-yeeb. eet-bah-nee meen fad-leek.* Okay. Follow me please.)

Salesperson: **'ulaa'ika kul aj-jakiiTaat 'indanaa.** (*oo-lah-ee-kah kool ah-jah-kee-tat een-dah-nah.* Those are all the jackets we have.)

Omar: **'uHibbu haa'ulaa'ii aj-jakiiTaat.** (*oo-hee-boo hah-oo-lah-ee ah-jah-kee-tat.* I like these jackets.)

Salesperson: **'anaa muwaafiq. 'innahaa jamiila jiddan.** (*ah-nah moo-wah-feek. ee-nah-hah jah-mee-lah jee-dan.* I agree. They are very beautiful.)

Omar: **'uriidu 'an 'ujarrib haadhihi.** (*oo-ree-doo an oo-jah-reeb hah-zee-hee.* I would like to try on this one.)

Salesperson: **fawran. hal turiidu lawn khaaS?** (*faw-ran. hal too-ree-doo lah-wen kass?* Right away. Are you looking for any particular color?)

Omar: **'uriidu dhaalika al-lawn.** (*oo-ree-doo zah-lee-kah ah-lah-wen.* I want that color.)

Words to Know

naw'	nah-weh	type/kind
yatba'u	yat-bah-oo	following
'itba'	eet-bah	follow (imperative)
'itba'nii	eet-bah-nee	follow me
muwaafiq	moo-wah-feek	agree
jamiil	jah-meel	beautiful (M)
jamiila	jah-mee-lah	beautiful (F)
'ujarrib	oo-jah-reeb	to try (I/me)
lawn	lah-wen	color
khaaS	kass	particular (M)
khaaSSa	kah-sah	particular (F)

Comparing Merchandise

Debating between two or more comparable items? In this section, you discover how to evaluate comparable (and incomparable) items based on a variety of important criteria, such as price, quality, and durability.

Comparing two or more items

Adjectives are the linguistic backbone that allow for comparisons between different items, products, or goods. Table 6-2 lists some of the most common adjectives. Table 6-3 lists the comparative forms of those adjectives.

Table 6-2	Common Arabic Adjectives	
Adjective	*Pronunciation*	*Translation*
Kabiir	*kah-beer*	big
Saghiir	*sah-gheer*	small
Hasan	*hah-san*	good
suu'	*sooh*	bad
rakhiiS	*rah-kees*	cheap
ghalii	*ghah-lee*	expensive
sarii'	*sah-reeh*	fast
baTii'	*bah-teeh*	slow
thaqiil	*tah-keel*	heavy
khafiif	*kah-feef*	light
jamiil	*jah-meel*	pretty
bashii'	*bah-sheeh*	ugly
ba'iid	*bah-eed*	far
qariib	*qah-reeb*	near
jadiid	*jah-deed*	new
qadiim	*qah-deem*	old

Table 6-3	Comparative Forms of Common Adjectives	
Comparative	**Pronunciation**	**Translation**
'akbar	ak-bar	bigger
'aSghar	ass-ghar	smaller
'aHsan	ah-san	better
'aswa'	as-wah	worse
'arkhas	ar-kas	cheaper
'aghlaa	ag-lah	more expensive
'asra'	ass-rah	faster
'abTa	ab-tah	slower
'athqal	at-kal	heavier
'akhfaa	ak-fah	lighter
'ajmal	aj-mal	prettier
'absha'	ab-shah	uglier
'ab'ad	ab-ad	farther
'aqrab	ak-rab	nearer
'ajadd	ah-jad	newer
'aqdam	ak-dam	older

Similar to English, the comparative forms of adjectives always follow this pattern:

> noun + adjective comparative form + preposition **min** (*meen;* than) + second adjective

It's essential that you include the preposition **min** right after every comparative adjective. In addition, all nouns being compared need to be defined by attaching to them the definite article prefix **al-.**

Here are some common examples of comparative sentences using the adjective forms:

- ✔ **al-bint 'akbar min al-walad.** (*al-bee-net ak-bar meen al-wah-lad;* The girl is bigger than the boy.)

- ✔ **at-tilifizyuun 'aghlaa min al-midyaa'.** (*ah-tee-lee-fee-zee-yoon ag-lah meen al-meed-yah;* The television is more expensive than the radio.)

- ✔ **as-sayyaara 'asra' min as-shaaHina.** (*ah-sah-yah-rah as-rah meen ah-shah-hee-nah;* The car is faster than the bus.)

- ✔ **aj-jakiiTa 'arkhas min al-qamiis.** (*ah-jah-kee-tah ar-kas meen al-qah-mees;* The jacket is cheaper than the shirt.)

When forming these types of sentences, you may add demonstratives to be even more specific. Here are examples of comparative sentences used in conjunction with demonstratives:

- ✔ **haadhihi al-bint 'akbar min dhaalika al-walad.** (*hah-zee-hee al-bee-net ak-bar meen zah-lee-kah al-wah-lad;* This girl is bigger than that boy.)

- ✔ **haadhihi as-sayyaaraat 'asra' min 'tilka as-shaahinaat.** (*hah-zee-hee ah-sah-yah-rat as-rah meen teel-kah ah-shah-hee-nat;* These cars are faster than those buses.)

- ✔ **tilka al-'imra'a 'ajmal min dhaalika ar-rajul.** (*teel-kah al-eem-rah-ah aj-mal meen zah-lee-kah ah-rah-jool;* That woman is prettier than that man.)

- ✔ **haadhaa al-walad 'akbar min 'ulaa'ika al-banaat.** (*hah-zah al-wah-lad ak-bar meen oo-lah-ee-kah al-bah-nat;* This boy is bigger than those girls.)

Notice in the examples that the adjective comparative form remains constant whether the nouns being compared are a combination of singular/singular, singular/plural, or plural/plural. In other words, the adjective comparatives are neutral: They remain the same regardless of both gender and number.

Picking out the best item

You use a *superlative* to say something is the "best," "brightest," "fastest," "cleanest," or "cheapest." Basically, a superlative in Arabic is nothing more than the comparative form of the adjective! The only difference is that comparatives include the preposition **min** (than) and superlatives don't include any preposition. For example, to tell someone, "This is the biggest house," you say **haadhaa 'akbar manzil** (*hah-zah ak-bar man-zeel*).

The biggest differences between superlatives and comparatives are:

- ✔ The superlative adjective always comes before the noun.
- ✔ When expressing a superlative, the noun is always undefined.

Here are some examples of superlative sentences:

- ✔ **haadhihi 'ajmal bint.** (*hah-zee-hee aj-mal bee-net;* This is the prettiest girl.)
- ✔ **dhaalika 'ab'ad dukkaan.** (*zah-lee-kah ab-ad doo-kan;* That is the farthest store.)

If you switch the order of the words to demonstrative + noun + superlative, be sure to define the noun. That's the only other way you can construct a superlative sentence. For example:

- ✔ **haadhihi al-bint 'ajmal.** (*hah-zee-hee al-bee-net aj-mal;* This girl is the prettiest.)
- ✔ **dhaalika ad-dukaan 'ab'ad.** (*zah-lee-kah ah-doo-kan ab-ad;* That store is the farthest.)

Here's a conversation you might have when shopping around for the best option:

Salesman: **SabaaH an-nuur wa marHaba 'ilaa ad-dukkaan al-iliktroniyaat.** (*Sah-bah ah-noor wah mar-hah-bah ee-lah ah-doo-kan al-ee-leek-troo-nee-yat.* Good morning and welcome to the electronics store.)

Adam: **shukran. 'anaa 'abHathu 'an muSaw-wira.** (*shook-ran. ah-nah ab-hah-thoo an moo-sah-wee-rah.* Thank you. I am looking for a camera.)

Salesman: **hal tabHathu 'an naw' mu'ayyin?** (*hal tab-hah-thoo an nah-weh moo-ah-yeen?* Are you looking for a particular model?)

Adam: **'abHath 'an 'aHsan muSawwira.** (*ab-hath an ah-san moo-sah-wee-rah.* I'm looking for the best camera.)

Salesman: **Tayyib. 'indanaa haadhaa an-naw' bi alwaan mutaghayyira.** (*Tah-yeeb. een-dah-nah hah-zah ah-nah-weh bee al-wan moo-tah-ghah-yee-rah.* Okay. We have this model with different colors.)

Adam: **hal 'indakum naw' 'aakhar?** (*hal een-dah-koom nah-weh ah-kar?* Do you have another model?)

Salesman: **na'am. haadhaa an-naw' ath-thaanii mashhuur ma'a az-zabaa'in.** (*nah-am. hah-zah ah-nah-weh ah-thah-nee mash-hoor mah-ah ah-zah-bah-een.* Yes. This second model is popular with customers.)

Adam: **'ay naw' 'aHsan?** (*ay nah-weh ah-san?* Which is the best model?)

Salesman: **an-naw' ath-thaanii 'aHsan min an-naw' al-awwal.** (*ah-nah-weh ah-thah-nee ah-san meen ah-nah-weh al-ah-wal.* The second model is better than the first model.)

Adam: **'uriidu 'an 'ashtarii an-naw' ath-thaanii min faDlik.** (*oo-ree-doo an ash-tah-ree ah-nah-weh ah-thah-nee meen fad-leek.* I'd like to buy the second model please.)

Salesman: **'ikhtiyaar mumtaaz!** (*eek-tee-yar moom-taz!* Excellent selection!)

Words to Know

mu'ayyin	moo-ah-yeen	particular (M)
mu'ayyina	moo-ah-yee-nah	particular (F)
mutaghayyir	moo-tah-ghah-yeer	different (M)
mutaghayyira	moo-tah-ghah-yee-rah	different (F)
zabaa'in	zah-bah-een	customers
'ikhtiyaar	eek-tee-yar	selection (M)
'ikthiyaara	eek-tee-yah-rah	selection (F)

Shopping for Clothes

For many people, one of the most essential items to shop for is **malaabis** (*mah-lah-bees;* clothes). Table 6-4 lists some basic articles of clothing and accessories you should know.

Table 6-4	Clothing and Accessories	
Arabic	*Pronunciation*	*Translation*
sirwaal	*seer-wal*	pants (S)
saraawiil	*sah-rah-weel*	pants (P)
qamiis	*qah-mees*	shirt
'aqmisa	*ak-mee-sah*	shirts
mi'Taf	*meeh-taf*	coat
ma'aaTif	*mah-ah-teef*	coats
kaswa	*kass-wah*	dress

Arabic	*Pronunciation*	*Translation*
'aksiwa	*ak-see-wah*	dresses
jallaaba	*jah-lah-bah*	Arab dress
jallaabaat	*jah-lah-bat*	Arab dresses
Hizaam	*hee-zam*	belt
'aHzima	*ah-zee-mah*	belts
qubba'a	*koo-bah-ah*	hat
qubba'aat	*koo-bah-at*	hats
jawrab	*jaw-rab*	sock
jawaarib	*jah-wah-reeb*	socks
Hidaa'	*hee-dah*	shoe
'aHdiya	*ah-dee-yah*	shoes
khaatim	*kah-teem*	ring
saa'a	*sah-ah*	watch

An important consideration when you're out shopping for **malaabis** is **al-Hajem** (*al-hah-jem;* size). The four standard clothes sizes are:

✔ **Saghiir** (*sah-gheer;* small) (American size [Men's]: 34–36; American size [Women's]: 6–8)

✔ **waSat** (*wah-sat;* medium) (American size [Men's]: 38–40; American size [Women's]: 10–12)

✔ **kabiir** (*kah-beer;* large) (American size [Men's]: 42–44; American size [Women's]: 14–16)

✔ **zaa'id kabiir** (*zah-eed kah-beer;* extra large) (American size [Men's]: 46 and above; American size [Women's]: 18–20)

Another important consideration in clothes shopping is the **lawn** (*lah-wen;* color). Because **'alwaan** (*al-wan;* colors) are adjectives that describe nouns, a **lawn** must always agree with the noun in terms of gender. How do you know whether a noun is feminine or masculine? In about 80 percent of the cases, feminine nouns end with a **fatHa**, or the "ah" sound. For the rest, you must look up the word in the **qaamuus** (*qah-moos;* dictionary) to determine its gender. The masculine and feminine forms of some common colors appear in Table 6-5.

Table 6-5		Basic Colors in Arabic		
Color (M)	*Pronunciation*	*Color (F)*	*Pronunciation*	*Translation*
'abyaD	*ab-yad*	**bayDaa'**	*bay-dah*	white
'aswad	*ass-wad*	**sawdaa'**	*saw-dah*	black
'aHmar	*ah-mar*	**Hamraa'**	*ham-rah*	red
'akhDar	*ak-dar*	**khaDraa'**	*kad-rah*	green
'azraq	*az-rak*	**zarqaa'**	*zar-qah*	blue
'aSfar	*ass-far*	**Safraa'**	*saf-rah*	yellow

Chapter 7

Making Leisure a Top Priority

- -

In This Chapter

▶ Experiencing the culture of a museum

▶ Taking in a movie

▶ Touring religious sites

▶ Playing sports

▶ Heading outside

- -

This chapter is all about leisure, whether going out in the **madiina** (*mah-dee-nah;* city), picking up a game with friends, or hitting the beach.

Visiting Museums

A **ziyaara** (*zee-yah-rah;* visit) to a **matHaf** (*mat-haf;* museum) can be a wonderful experience as long as you follow a number of **qawaa'id** (*qah-wah-eed;* rules). These **qawaa'id** ensure that your experience and the experiences of others at the **matHaf** are **jamiila** (*jah-mee-lah;* pleasant).

Arab scholars and Western civilization

Many of the works of the ancient Greek masters, such as Aristotle and Plato, were preserved by Islamic scholars when Europe was plunged into the Dark Ages (from about the Fifth through the Tenth centuries). Muslim scholars throughout the Muslim world, in Cordoba, Spain, and elsewhere, translated gargantuan amounts of texts from Greek and Latin into Arabic. They studied these texts extensively and added a significant amount to the pool of knowledge. Thanks to the work of these Muslim scholars, much of the knowledge that serves as the basis of Western thought and civilization was preserved. In fact, while Europe was in the Dark Ages, Islam went through a revival and renaissance period not experienced anywhere else in the world.

When visiting a **matHaf,** here are some phrases you may use or see posted:

- ✔ **hayyaa binaa 'ilaa al-matHaf al-yawm.** (*hah-yah bee-nah ee-lah al-mat-haf al-yah-oum.* Let's go to the museum today.)

- ✔ **'ayna al-matHaf?** (*eh-yeh-nah al-mat-haf?* Where is the museum located?)

- ✔ **wa bikam biTaaqat ad-dukhuul?** (*wah bee-kam bee-tah-kat ah-doo-kool?* And how much is the entry ticket?)

- ✔ **mataa yaftaHu al-matHaf?** (*mah-tah yaf-tah-hoo al-mat-haf?* When does the museum open?)

- ✔ **al-matHaf yaftaHu ma'a as-saa'a ath-thaamina fii aS-SabaaH.** (*al-mat-haf yaf-tah-hoo mah-ah ah-sah-ah ah-thah-mee-nah fee ah-sah-bah.* The museum opens at 8:00 in the morning.)

- ✔ **Suwar mamnuu'a.** (*soo-war mam-noo-ah;* Taking pictures is prohibited.)

- ✔ **malaabis munaasiba Daruuriya** (*mah-lah-bees moo-naa-see-bah dah-roo-ree-yah;* Proper attire required.)

Words to Know

Ziyaaratukum	zee-yah-rah-too-koom	your visit (MP)
tamtii'	tam-teeh	entertainment
mutamatti'a	moo-tah-mah-tee-ah	entertaining
jiddan	jee-dan	very
ra'aa	rah-ah	saw
fann	fah-n	art
taSwiir	tah-sweer	painting
rasm	rah-sem	drawing/carving
zaliij	zah-leej	marble
jamiil	jah-meel	pretty/beautiful
jawla	jah-ou-lah	tour
khalfa	kal-fah	around
dukhuul	doo-kool	entrance
khuruuj	koo-rooj	exit
fataHa	fah-tah-hah	to open
yaftaHu	yaf-tah-hoo	will open

Going to the Movies

Going to see a **shariiT siinimaa'ii** (*sha-reet see-nee-mah-ee;* movie) in a **maSraH siiniima'ii** (*mas-rah see-nee-mah-ee;* movie theater) is a very popular pastime for people in the Middle East. Here are some popular movie genres:

- ✔ **mughaamara** (*moo-ghah-mah-rah;* action/ adventure)
- ✔ **maSraHiyya** (*mas-rah-hee-yah;* comedy)
- ✔ **draamii** (*drah-mee;* drama)
- ✔ **ru'aat al-baqar** (*roo-aht al-bah-kar;* western)
- ✔ **wathaa'iqii** (*wah-tha-ee-kee;* documentary)
- ✔ **rusuum al-mutaHarrika** (*roo-soom al-moo-tah-hah-ree-kah;* cartoon)

Most of the movies shown in these **maSraH siiniima'ii** are actually the original versions of American films with **tarjamat al-Hiiwaar** (*tar-jah-mat al-hee-war;* subtitles).

The verb most commonly associated with going to the movies is **dhahaba** (*za-hah-bah;* to go). Using the conjugations that follow, you can say

dhahabtu 'ilaa al-maSraH as-siiniima'ii (*za-hab-too ee-lah al-mas-rah ah-see-nee-mah-ee;* I went to the movie theater.)

yadhhabu 'ilaa al-maSraH as-siiniima'ii (*yaz-hah-boo ee-lah al-mas-rah ah-see-nee-mah-ee;* He is going to the movies.)

Table 7-1 shows the past tense of "to go"; Table 7-2 shows the present tense.

Table 7-1	The Past Tense of the Verb *dhahaba* (To Go)	
Form	**Pronunciation**	**Translation**
'anaa dhahabtu	*ah-nah za-hab-too*	I went
'anta dhahabta	*ahn-tah za-hab-tah*	You went (MS)
'anti dhahabtii	*ahn-tee za-hab-tee*	You went (FS)
huwa dhaaba	*hoo-wah za-hah-bah*	He went
hiya dhahabat	*hee-yah za-hah-bat*	She went
naHnu dhahabnaa	*nah-noo za-hab-naa*	We went
'antum dhahabtum	*ahn-toom za-hab-toom*	You went (MP)
'antunna dhahabtunna	*ahn-too-nah za-hab-too-nah*	You went (FP)
hum dhahabuu	*hoom za-hah-boo*	They went (MP)
hunna dhahabna	*hoo-nah za-hab-nah*	They went (FP)
antumaa dhahabtumaa	*ahn-too-mah za-hab-too-mah*	You went (dual/MP/FP)
humaa dhahabaa	*hoo-mah za-hah-bah*	They went (dual/MP)
humaa dhahabataa	*hoo-mah za-hah-bah-tah*	They went (dual/FP)

Table 7-2	The Present Tense of the Verb *dhahaba* (To Go)	
Form	**Pronunciation**	**Translation**
'anaa 'adhhabu	*ah-nah az-hah-boo*	I am going
'anta tadhhabu	*ahn-tah taz-hah-boo*	You are going (MS)

(continued)

Table 7-2 (continued)

Form	Pronunciation	Translation
'anti tadhhabiina	ahn-tee taz-hah-bee-nah	You are going (FS)
huwa yadhhabu	hoo-wah yaz-hah-boo	He is going
hiya tadhhabu	hee-yah taz-hah-boo	She is going
naHnu nadhhabu	nah-noo naz-hah-boo	We are going
'antum tadhhabuuna	ahn-toom taz-hah-boo-nah	You are going (MP)
'antunna tadhhabna	ahn-too-nah taz-hab-nah	You are going (FP)
hum yadhhabuuna	hoom yaz-hah-boo-nah	They are going (MP)
hunna yadhhabna	hoo-nah yaz-hab-nah	They are going (FP)
antumaa tadhhabaani	ahn-too-mah taz-hah-bah-nee	You are going (dual/MP/FP)
humaa yadhhabaani	hoo-mah yaz-hah-bah-nee	They are going (dual/MP)
humaa tadhhabaani	hoo-mah taz-hah-bah-nee	They are going (dual/FP)

Some other helpful movie-related words and phrases are:

- **mumathil** (*moo-mah-theel*; actor)

- **mumathila** (*moo-mah-thee-lah*; actress)

- **mudiir** (*moo-deer*; director)

- **mushaahid** (*moo-sha-heed*; spectator) (MS)

- **mushaahida** (*moo-sha-hee-dah*; spectator) (FS)

- **'anaa 'uriidu 'an 'adhhab 'ilaa al-maSraH as-siiniima'ii.** (*ah-nah oo-ree-doo ann az-hab ee-lah al-mas-rah ah-see-nee-mah-ee.* I would like to go to the movie theater.)

✔ **mataa sayabda'u ash-shariiT?** (*mah-tah sah-yab-dah-oo ah-sha-reet?* When does the movie begin?)

✔ **'ay shariiT sayal'abu fii al-maSraH al-yawm?** (*aiy sha-reet sah-yal-ah-boo fee al-mas-rah al-yah-oum?* Which movie is going to be playing today?)

Touring Religious Sites

If you're in a Middle Eastern or Arab city, be sure to check out a **masjid** (*mas-jeed;* mosque). The largest **masaajid** (*mah-sah-jeed;* mosques) in the Muslim world are located in Mecca and Medina, Saudi Arabia, and in Casablanca, Morocco.

A few rules to keep in mind

When visiting **masaajid**, you must follow certain **qawaa'id** (rules):

✔ **If you're Muslim,** you're allowed to walk into any **masjid** you like; but before entering, you must remove your shoes and say the **shahada** (*shah-hah-dah;* religious prayer): **laa 'ilaaha 'illaa allah wa muHammad rasuul allah** (*lah ee-lah-hah ee-lah ah-lah wah moo-hah-mad rah-sool ah-lah;* There is no god but God and Muhammad is his Prophet.).

✔ **If you're non-Muslim,** entry into a **masjid** is sometimes forbidden, whether you're in the Middle East, the United States, or anywhere around the world. However, certain mosques, such as the **masjid Hassan II** in Casablanca, have designated wings that are open to both Muslims and non-Muslims. These wings are set aside more as exhibition rooms than as religious or prayer rooms, so you're allowed to enter them, but you still must remove your **Hidaa'** (*hee-dah;* shoes).

The word **masjid** comes from the verb **sajada** (*sah-jah-dah*), which means "to prostrate" or "to kneel." Another word for "mosque" is **jaami'** (*jah-meeh*), which comes from the word **jama'a** (*jah-mah-ah;* to gather). So the Arabic words for "mosque" are related to what one actually does in the mosque, which is to gather in a religious setting and pray.

The Hajj

One of the most popular events during the year for Muslims is the **Hajj** (*haj*), which is the pilgrimage to Mecca in Saudi Arabia. The **Hajj,** which generally lasts for five days, takes place once a year and is actually one of the five pillars of Islam.

As soon as the **Hajjaaj** (*hah-jaj;* pilgrims) arrive in Mecca, they must shed all their worldly clothing and possessions and change into sandals and a simple **ihram** (*eeh-ram*), which basically consists of a white cloth wrapped around the body. The logic behind wearing only the **ihram** is that every **Hajjaaj** is equal before God, and because no difference exists between a king and a beggar during the **Hajj,** everyone must wear the same thing.

After they don the **ihram,** the **Hajjaaj** begin a ritual known as the **Tawaf** (*tah-waf;* to turn), in which they walk around the **ka'ba** (*kah-bah*), a cubelike structure located in the middle of the **masjid al-Haraam** (*mas-jeed al-hah-ram;* The Sacred Mosque of Mecca). According to the Koran and other religious texts, the **ka'ba** was built by the Prophet Abraham for the purpose of worship. The **Hajjaaj** must circle the **ka'ba** seven times in an anti-clockwise manner. After the **Tawaf,** the **Hajjaaj** walk to the hills of Safa and Marwah before going to the hill of Arafat, then to the city of Mina, before returning to the **ka'ba** for a final **Tawaf.**

A man who has completed the **Hajj** is called **al-Hajj** (*al-haj*), and a woman who has done the **Hajj** is called **al-Hajja** (*al-hah-jah*).

 Saudi Arabian law prohibits non-Muslims from entering Mecca.

Sporting an Athletic Side

I don't know about you, but I love playing **riyaaDa** (*ree-yah-dah;* sports), whether it's an individual sport such as **al-ghuulf** (*al-ghoo-lef;* golf) or a team sport like **kurat al-qadam** (*koo-rat al-qah-dam;* soccer).

kurat al-qadam is one of the most popular sports among Arabic-speaking people because it's a **riyaaDa mushaahada** (*ree-yah-dah moo-sha-hah-dah;* spectator sport). In a typical **mubaara** (*moo-bah-rah;* game), you will use the following words:

- **fariiq** (*fah-reek;* team)
- **mal'ab** (*mah-lab;* stadium)
- **natiija** (*nah-tee-jah;* score)
- **fawz** (*fah-wez;* win)
- **khasar** (*kah-sar;* loss)
- **khata'** (*kah-tah;* foul)
- **Hakam** (*hah-kam;* referee)
- **malaabis riyaaDiyya** (*mah-lah-bees ree-yah-dee-yah;* uniforms)
- **kura** (*koo-rah;* ball)
- **laa'ib** (*lah-eeb;* player) (MS)
- **laa'iba** (*lah-ee-bah;* player) (FS)

Here are some other favorite sports:

- **sibaaHa** (*see-bah-hah;* swimming)
- **furusiiyya** (*foo-roo-see-yah;* horseback riding)

- ✔ **kurat aT-Taa'ira** (*koo-rat ah-tah-ee-rah;* volleyball)

- ✔ **kurat as-salla** (*koo-rat ah-sah-lah;* basketball)

- ✔ **kurat al-miDrab** (*koo-rat al-meed-rab;* tennis)

- ✔ **daraaja** (*dah-rah-jah;* cycling)

- ✔ **tazaHluq** (*tah-zah-look;* skiing)

- ✔ **tazalluj** (*tah-zah-looj;* ice skating)

- ✔ **jumbaaz** (*joo-meh-baz;* gymnastics)

- ✔ **siibaaq as-sayaara** (*see-bah-kah ah-sah-yah-rah;* racecar driving)

One of the most common verbs used with sports and other recreational activities is **la'aba** (*lah-ah-bah;* play). Because the verb **la'aba** is commonly used and important, knowing how to conjugate it in both the past and the present tenses is a good idea. Tables 7-3 and 7-4 show you how.

Table 7-3	The Past Tense of the Verb *la'aba* (To Play)	
Form	*Pronunciation*	*Translation*
'anaa la'abtu	*ah-nah lah-ahb-too*	I played
'anta la'abta	*ahn-tah lah-ahb-tah*	You played (MS)
'anti la'abti	*ahn-tee lah-ahb-tee*	You played (FS)
Huwa la'aba	*hoo-wah lah-ah-bah*	He played
Hiya la'abat	*hee-yah lah-ah-bat*	She played
naHnu la'abnaa	*nah-noo lah-ahb-naa*	We played
'antum la'abtum	*ahn-toom lah-ahb-toom*	You played (MP)
'antunna la'abtunna	*ahn-too-nah lah-ahb-too-nah*	You played (FP)
Hum la'abuu	*hoom lah-ah-boo*	They played (MP)

Form	Pronunciation	Translation
Hunna la'abna	*hoo-nah lah-ahb-nah*	They played (FP)
antumaa la'abtumaa	*ahn-too-mah lah-ahb-too-mah*	You played (dual/MP/FP)
Humaa la'abaa	*hoo-mah lah-ah-bah*	They played (dual/MP)
Humaa la'abataa	*hoo-mah lah-ah-bah-tah*	They played (dual/FP)

Table 7-4	The Present Tense of the Verb *yal'abu* (To Play)	
Form	**Pronunciation**	**Translation**
'anaa 'al'abu	*ah-nah al-ah-boo*	I am playing
'anta tal'abu	*ahn-tah tal-ah-boo*	You are playing (MS)
'anti tal'abiina	*ahn-tee tal-ah-bee-nah*	You are playing (FS)
Huwa yal'abu	*hoo-wah yal-ah-boo*	He is playing
Hiya tal'abu	*hee-yah tal-ah-boo*	She is playing
naHnu nal'abu	*nah-noo nal-ah-boo*	We are playing
'antum tal'abuuna	*ahn-toom tal-ah-boo-nah*	You are playing (MP)
'antunna tal'abna	*ahn-too-nah tal-ahb-nah*	You are playing (FP)
hum yal'abuuna	*hoom yal-ah-boo-nah*	They are playing (MP)
hunna yal'abna	*hoo-nah yal-ahb-nah*	They are playing (FP)
antumaa tal'abaani	*ahn-too-mah tal-ah-bah-nee*	You are playing (dual/MP/FP)
Humaa yal'abaani	*hoo-mah yal-ah-bah-nee*	They are playing (dual/MP)
Humaa tal'abaani	*hoo-mah tal-ah-bah-nee*	They are playing (dual/FP)

Use the verb **la'aba** or **yal'abu** followed by the sport or activity you're playing. For example, you may say

'anaa 'al'abu kurat as-salla. (I am playing basketball.)

hiya la'abat kurat al-miDrab. (She played tennis.)

Another important phrase commonly used relating to sports and other fun activities is **hayyaa binaa** (_hah-yah bee-nah;_ Let's go). You'll often hear friends telling each other **hayyaa binaa** followed by the activity or location of the activity, such as **hayyaa binaa 'ilaa mal'ab kurat al-qadam** (_hah-yah bee-nah ee-lah mal-ahb koo-rat al-aah-dam;_ Let's go to the soccer field).

The following conversation gives you some important phrases in case you want to get a friend to play **kurat al-qadam** with you:

Karim: **hayyaa nal'ab kurat al-qadam ghadan.** (_hah-yah nah-lab koo-rat al-qah-dam ghah-dan._ Let's go play soccer tomorrow.)

Kamal: **haadhihi fikra mumtaaza.** (_hah-zee-hee feek-rah moom-tah-zah._ That's an excellent idea.)

Karim: **'ayy saa'a?** (_ay sah-ah?_ At what time?)

Kamal: **hal as-saa'a al-khaamisa tuwaafiquka?** (_hal ah-sah-ah al-kah-mee-sah too-wah-fee-koo-kah?_ Does 5:00 work for you?)

Karim: **na'am. as-saa'a al-khaamisa muwaafiqa. 'ayna sa-nal'ab?** (_nah-am. ah-sah-ah al-kah-mee-sah moo-wah-fee-qah. eh-yeh-nah sa-nah-lab?_ Yes. 5:00 works for me. Where are we going to play?)

Kamal: **fii mal'ab al-madrasa.** (_fee mah-lab al-mad-rah-sah._ In the school stadium.)

Karim: **mumtaaz! hal 'indaka kura?** (_moom-tahz! hal een-dah-kah koo-rah?_ Excellent! Do you have a ball?)

Kamal: **na'am 'indii kura. wa laakin laysa 'indii malaabis riyaaDiyya.** (*nah-am een-dee koo-rah. wah lah-keen lah-yeh-sah een-dee mah-lah-bees ree-yah-dee-yah.* Yes, I have a ball. But I don't have any uniforms.)

Karim: **laa sha'na lanaa bidhaalika. lam naHtaaj bi al-malaabis riyaaDiyya.** (*lah sha-nah lah-nah bee-zah-lee-kah. lam nah-taj bee al-mah-lah-bees ree-yah-dee-yah.* That's not a big deal. We really don't need uniforms.)

Going to the Beach

Whether you go to the **shaaTi'** (*shah-teeh;* beach) with your **'aSdiqaa'** (*ass-dee-qah;* friends) or your **'usra** (*oos-rah;* family), it's a really great place to have a fun time! Here are some useful words for the beach:

- ✔ **malaabis as-sibaaHa** (*mah-lah-bees ah-see-bah-hah;* bathing suit)
- ✔ **dihaan shamsii** (*dee-han shah-meh-see;* sunscreen)
- ✔ **shams** (*shah-mes;* sun)
- ✔ **saHaab** (*sah-hab;* cloud)
- ✔ **muHiiT** (*moo-heet;* ocean)
- ✔ **miDalla** (*mee-dah-lah;* beach umbrella)
- ✔ **ramla** (*rah-meh-lah;* sand)
- ✔ **mooja** (*moo-jah;* wave)

hayyaa binaa 'ilaa ash-shaaTi'! (*hah-yah bee-nah ee-lah ah-shah-teeh!* Let's go to the beach!)

Playing Musical Instruments

No matter where you come from or what languages you speak, **moosiiqaa** (*moo-see-qah;* music) has the power to break down barriers and bring people closer together. Popular **aalaat moosiiqiyya** (*ah-lat moo-see-kee-yah;* musical instruments) include:

- ✔ **biiyaano** (*bee-yah-noo;* piano)
- ✔ **qiithaar** (*kee-thar;* guitar)
- ✔ **kamanja** (*kah-mah-neh-jah;* violin)
- ✔ **Tabl** (*tah-bel;* drums)
- ✔ **fluut** (*feh-loot;* flute)
- ✔ **buuq** (*book;* trumpet)
- ✔ **saaksuufuun** (*sak-soo-foon;* saxophone)

In order to say that someone plays a particular instrument, use the **muDaari'** form of the verb **yal'abu.** For example **yal'abu al-qiithaar** means "He plays the guitar" or "He is playing the guitar".

Middle Eastern music is one of the most popular types of music in the world. It is characterized by a special kind of string instrument called the **'uud** (*ood*) that has 12 strings and a round hollow body. The **'uud** is generally accompanied by a number of percussion instruments, such as the regular drum and the special **Tabla** (*tah-beh-lah*) that keeps the beat and adds extra flavor to the serenading of the **'uud.**

Popular Hobbies

Besides **riyaaDa** and **moosiiqaa,** you may enjoy a number of other types of hobbies. Do you consider **qiraa'a** (*kee-rah-ah;* reading) a **hiwaaya** (*hee-wah-yah;* hobby)? Perhaps you're creative and like **rasm** (*rah-sem;* drawing) or **fakhaar** (*fah-kar;* pottery)?

Some other popular hobbies include:

- ✔ **waraq al-la'ib** (*wah-rak ah-lah-eeb;* cards)
- ✔ **raqS** (*rah-kes;* dancing)
- ✔ **shaTranj** (*sha-teh-rah-nej;* chess)
- ✔ **Hiyaaka** (*hee-yah-kah;* knitting)
- ✔ **shi'r** (*shee-ar;* poetry)

When you want to discuss hobbies and personal activities, you often use the verb **la'aba.** For example, you say **la'abtu kurat al-qadam** (*lah-ab-too koo-rat al-qah-dam;* I played soccer) or **la'aba al-kamanja** (*lah-ah-bah al-kah-mah-neh-jah;* He played the violin). Here are some other example sentences that pair activities with the verb **la'aba:**

- ✔ **la'abat shaTranj.** (*lah-ah-bat sha-teh-rah-nej;* She played chess.)
- ✔ **la'abnaa kurat as-salla.** (*lah-ab-nah koo-rat ah-sah-lah;* We played basketball.)
- ✔ **la'abaa waraq al-la'ib.** (*lah-ah-bah wah-rak ah-lah-eeb;* They played cards.) (dual/MP/FP)

Chapter 8

When You Gotta Work

In This Chapter

▶ Finding a job that's right for you

▶ Interacting with coworkers

▶ Using the phone

*W*hether you're looking for a job or just need to talk with your coworkers, this chapter has the phrases for you. I also give you basic phone vocabulary and tell you how to send letters, e-mails, and faxes.

Landing a Job

If you're looking for **'amal** (*ah-mal;* work/job) or trying to decide what **mihna** (*meeh-nah;* profession) to pursue, this section is for you.

One of the first things to keep in mind when you go about your job search is that you need to find an **'amal** that suits your particular **maSlaHaat** (*mas-lah-hat;* interests) and **mahaaraat** (*mah-hah-rat;* skills). You may want to start your search by talking to **'aSdiqaa'** (*ass-dee-qah;* friends) or asking around at your local **jam'iyya** (*jam-ee-yah;* university). Also, you're likely to find listings in the following:

▸ **jariidaat** (*jah-ree-dat;* newspapers)

▸ **ma'luumaat** (*mah-loo-mat;* classified ads)

As you search, make sure you find out as much as possible about a potential **mustakhdim** (*moos-tak-deem;* employer). When you're able to secure an interview with a **sharika** (*shah-ree-kah;* company), here's a list of things you may want to find out about your potential **mustakhdim:**

- ✔ **'adad al-'ummaal** (*ah-dad al-oo-mal;* number of employees)

- ✔ **Damaan aS-SaHHa** (*dah-man ah-sah-hah;* health insurance)

- ✔ **raatib** (*rah-teeb;* salary)

- ✔ **waqt al-'uTla** (*wah-ket al-oot-lah;* vacation time)

- ✔ **ta'aaqud** (*tah-ah-kood;* pension)

Here's how an interview might go:

Mary: **marHaban bika. tafaDDal min faDlik.** (*mar-hah-ban bee-kah. tah-fah-dal meen fad-leek.* Welcome. Please come in.)

Mark: **shukran li 'istiqbaalii.** (*shook-ran lee ees-teek-bah-lee.* Thank you for having me.)

Mary: **khuz maq'ad min faDlik.** (*kooz mak-ad meen fad-leek.* Please have a seat.)

Mark: **shukran.** (*shook-ran.* Thank you.)

Mary: **hal turiidu 'an tashraba shay'an?** (*hal too-ree-doo an tash-rah-bah shay-an?* Would you like anything to drink?)

Mark: **maa' min faDlik.** (*mah meen fad-leek.* Water please.)

Mary: **hal 'indaka 'as'ila 'an haadhihi al-waDHiifa?** (*hal een-dah-kah ass-ee-lah an hah-zee-hee al-wah-dee-fah?* Do you have any questions about this position?)

Mark: **na'am. kam min 'ummaal fii ash-sharika?** (*nah-am. kam meen oo-mal fee ah-shah-ree-kah?* Yes. How many employees are in the company?)

Mary: **'indanaa 'ishriin 'ummaal wa mudiir waaHid.** (*een-dah-nah eesh-reen oo-mal wah moo-deer wah-heed.* We have 20 employees and one director.)

Mark: **hal ash-sharika tuqaddim Damaan aS-SaHHa?** (*hal ah-shah-ree-kah too-qah-deem dah-man ah-sah-hah?* Does the company provide health insurance?)

Mary: **na'am. nuqaddim Damaan aS-SaHHa li kul muwaDHaf ba'da muddat thalaath 'ashhur fii al-'amal.** (*nah-am. noo-qah-deem dah-man ah-sah-hah lee kool moo-wah-daf bah-dah moo-dat thah-lath ash-hoor fee al-ah-mal.* Yes. We provide health insurance to every employee after a period of three months on the job.)

Mark: **raai'! wa hal hunaaka waqt li al-'uTla?** (*rah-eeh! wah hal hoo-nah-kah wah-ket lee al-oot-lah?* Great! And is there any vacation time?)

Mary: **Taba'an. hunaaka 'ishriin yawm li al-'uTla fii as-sana al-'uulaa. wa fii as-sana ath-thaaniya hunaaka thalaathiin yawm li al-'uTla.** (*tah-bah-an. hoo-nah-kah eesh-reen yah-oum lee al-oot-lah fee ah-sah-nah al-oo-lah. wah fee ah-sah-nah ah-thah-nee-yah hoo-nah-kah thah-lah-theen yah-oum lee al-oot-lah.* Of course. There are 20 days for vacation during the first year. And then during the second year there are 30 vacation days.)

Mark: **shukran jaziilan li haadhihi al-ma'luumaat.** (*shook-ran jah-zee-lan lee hah-zee-hee al-mah-loo-mat.* Thank you very much for this information.)

Words to Know

'istiqbaal	ess-teek-bal	host
maq'ad	mak-ad	seat
'as'ila	ass-ee-lah	questions
		continued

Words to Know (continued)

waDHiifa	wah-dee-fah	position
taqdiim	tak-deem	offering
tuqaddim	too-qah-deem	to offer
'ashhur	ash-hoor	months
ma'luuma	mah-loo-mah	information (S)
ma'luumaat	mah-loo-mat	information (P)

Managing the Office Environment

The **maktab** is an essential part of modern life. In most Arabic-speaking and Muslim countries, **'ummaal** (*ooh-mal;* workers) work from **al-'ithnayn** (*al-eeth-nah-yen;* Monday) until **al-jumu'a** (*al-joo-moo-ah;* Friday). Most **'ummaal** follow a standard **as-saa'a at-taasi'a 'ilaa al-khaamisa** (*ah-sah-ah ah-tah-see-ah ee-lah al-kah-mee-sah;* 9:00 to 5:00) schedule for workdays.

Although most **makaatib** (*mah-kah-teeb;* offices) around the world give their **'ummaaal** time for **ghadaa'** (*ghah-dah;* lunch), the duration depends on the employer and the country. For example, in the United States, it's not uncommon for an **'aamil** (*ah-meel;* worker) to eat her **ghadaa'** while sitting at her **maktab** (*mak-tab;* desk). On the other hand, in most Middle Eastern countries, an **'aamil** gets two hours for **ghadaa'** and is encouraged to eat his **ghadaa'** at his **manzil** (*man-zeel;* house) with his **'usra** (*oos-rah;* family).

Here are some key words and terms to help you navigate the workplace:

- ✔ **'amal** (*ah-mal;* work/job)
- ✔ **mihna** (*meeh-nah;* profession)
- ✔ **sharika** (*shah-ree-kah;* company)
- ✔ **sharika kabiira** (*shah-ree-kah kah-bee-rah;* large company)
- ✔ **sharika Saghiira** (*shah-ree-kah sah-ghee-rah;* small company)
- ✔ **ma'mal** (*mah-mal;* factory)
- ✔ **zubuun** (*zoo-boon;* client)
- ✔ **zabaa'in** (*zah-bah-een;* clients)

You can choose from many different kinds of **sharikaat** (*shah-ree-kat;* companies) to work for, including a **maSraf** (*mas-raf;* bank), a **sharikat al-Hisaab** (*shah-ree-kat al-hee-sab;* accounting firm), and a **sharikat al-qaanuun** (*shah-ree-kat al-qah-noon;* law firm). You also have many choices when it comes to **mihan** (*mee-han;* professions). Here are some popular **mihan:**

- ✔ **maSrafii** (*mas-rah-fee;* banker) (M)
- ✔ **maSrafiiya** (*mas-rah-fee-yah;* banker) (F)
- ✔ **rajul al-'a'maal** (*rah-jool al-ah-mal;* businessman)
- ✔ **'imra'at al-'a'maal** (*eem-rah-at al-ah-mal;* businesswoman)
- ✔ **muHaamiiy** (*moo-hah-mee;* lawyer)
- ✔ **shurTa** (*shoor-tah;* police officer)
- ✔ **rajul al-'iTfaa'** (*rah-jool al-eet-fah;* firefighter)

Most **sharikaat** have a lot of **'ummaal** with different responsibilities, and most **'ummaal** find themselves in **daa'iraat** (*dah-ee-rat;* divisions/groups/departments) within the **sharika.** Here are some of the common **daa'iraat** you may find in a **sharika:**

- **daa'irat al-Hisaab** (*dah-ee-rat al-hee-sab;* accounting department)

- **daa'irat al-'aswaaq** (*dah-ee-rat al-as-wak;* marketing department)

- **daa'irat al-qaanuun** (*dah-ee-rat al-qah-noon;* legal department)

- **daa'irat al-'ummaal** (*dah-ee-rat al-ooh-mal;* human resources department)

- **daa'irat az-zabaa'in** (*dah-ee-rat ah-zah-bah-een;* customer service department)

Interacting with your colleagues

Unless you're in a **mihna** that doesn't require you to interact with people face-to-face, you need to be able to get along with your **zumalaa'** (*zoo-mah-lah;* colleagues) at the **maktab:**

- **zamiil** (*zah-meel;* colleague) (MS)

- **zamiila** (*zah-mee-lah;* colleague) (FS)

- **zumalaat** (*zoo-mah-lat;* colleagues) (FP)

- **mudiir** (*moo-deer;* director) (MS)

- **mudiira** (*moo-dee-rah;* director) (FS)

- **mudiiruun** (*moo-dee-roon;* directors) (MP)

- **mudiiraat** (*moo-dee-rat;* directors) (FP)

- **ra'iis** (*rah-ees;* president) (MS)

- **ra'iisa** (*rah-ee-sah;* president) (FS)

- **ru'asaa'** (*roo-ah-sah;* presidents) (MP)

- **ru'asaat** (*roo-ah-sat;* presidents) (FP)

You can address people you work with in a number of different ways, such as based on rank, age, or gender. These categorizations may seem discriminatory in an American sense, but these terms actually carry the utmost respect for the person being referenced:

- ✔ Use **sayyidii** (*sah-yee-dee;* sir) to address the **mudiir** or someone with a higher rank than you.

- ✔ Use **sayiidatii** (*sah-yee-dah-tee;* madam) to address the **mudiira** or **ra'iisa**.

- ✔ Use **Sadiiqii** (*sah-dee-kee;* friend) to address a male colleague.

- ✔ Use **Sadiiqatii** (*sah-dee-qah-tee;* friend) to address a **zamiila**.

- ✔ Use **al-'akh** (*al-ak;* brother) to address a male coworker or colleague.

- ✔ Use **al-'ukht** (*al-oo-ket;* sister) to address a **zamiila**.

In Arabic culture, it's okay to address coworkers or people close to you as **'akh** (brother) or **'ukht** (sister) even though they may not be related to you.

Here are some phrases to help you interact cordially and politely with your **zumalaa':**

- ✔ **hal turiid musaa'ada?** (*hal too-reed moo-sah-ah-dah;* Do you need help?) (M)

- ✔ **hal turiidiina musaa'ada?** (*hal too-ree-dee-nah moo-sah-ah-dah;* Do you need help?) (F)

- ✔ **hal yumkin 'an 'usaa'iduka bii dhaalika?** (*hal yoom-keen an oo-sah-ee-doo-kah bee zah-lee-kah;* May I help you with that?) (M)

- ✔ **hal yumkin 'an 'usaa'idukii bii dhaalika?** (*hal yoom-keen an oo-sah-ee-doo-kee bee zah-lee-kah;* May I help you with that?) (F)

- ✔ **sa 'adhhab 'ilaa al-maT'am. hal turiid shay'an?** (*sah az-hab ee-lah al-mat-ham. hal too-reed shay-an;* I'm going to the cafeteria. Do you want anything?) (M)

- ✔ **sa 'adhhab 'ilaa al-maT'am. hal turiidiina shay'an?** (*sah az-hab ee-lah al-mat-ham. hal too-ree-dee-nah shay-an;* I'm going to the cafeteria. Do you want anything?) (F)

- **'indanaa 'ijtimaa' fii khams daqaa'iq.** (*een-dah-nah eej-tee-mah fee kah-mes dah-qah-eek;* We have a meeting in five minutes.)

- **az-zabuun saya'tii fii saa'a.** (*ah-zah-boon sah-yah-tee fee sah-ah;* The client will arrive in one hour.)

- **hal waSaluka bariidii al-'iliktroonii?** (*hal wah-sah-loo-kah bah-ree-dee al-ee-leek-troo-nee;* Did you get my e-mail?)

- **hal waSaluka khabaarii al-haatifiiy?** (*hal wah-sah-loo-kah kah-bah-ree al-hah-tee-fee;* Did you get my phone message?)

- **hal 'indaka qalam?** (*hal een-dah-kah qah-lam;* Do you have a pen?) (M)

- **hal 'indukii qalam?** (*hal een-doo-kee qah-lam;* Do you have a pen?) (F)

Writing reports is something most people have to do at the office. Here's a conversation you might have with your colleagues:

Omar: **hal katabta at-taqriir?** (*hal kah-tab-tah ah-tak-reer?* Did you write the report?)

Samir: **'anaa katabtu niSf at-taqriir, wa laakin 'uriidu musaa'adatuka li kitaabatuh.** (*ah-nah kah-tab-too nee-sef ah-tak-reer, wah lah-keen oo-ree-doo moo-sah-ah-dah-too-kah lee kee-tah-bah-tooh.* I wrote half of the report, but I need your help to finish writing it.)

Omar: **Tayyib, hayyaa binaa li al-'amaal. 'ayna turiidu 'an na'mal?** (*tah-yeeb, hay-yah bee-nah lee al-ah-mal. ay-nah too-ree-doo an nah-mal?* Okay, let's get to work. Where would you like us to work?)

Samir: **hayya binaa 'ilaa qaa'at al-'ijtimaa'.** (*hay-yah bee-nah ee-lah qah-at al-eej-tee-mah.* Let's go to the conference room.)

Omar: **hal turiidu haadhihi aS-Suura fii bidaayat 'aw nihaayat at-taqriir?** (*hal too-ree-doo hah-zee-hee ah-soo-rah fee bee-dah-yat aw nee-hah-yat ah-tak-reer?* Do you want this illustration in the beginning or end of the report?)

Samir: **'aDHunnu fii bidaayat at-taqriir 'aHsan.** (*ah-zoo-noo fee bee-dah-yat ah-tak-reer ah-san.* I believe in the beginning of the report is better.)

Omar: **hal naziid SafHa 'ukhraa 'aw haadhaa kaafiiyan?** (*hal nah-zeed saf-hah ook-rah aw hah-zah kah-fee-yan?* Should we add another page or is this enough?)

Samir: **haadhaa kaafiyan li al-'aan.** (*hah-zah kah-fee-yan lee al-an.* This is enough for now.)

Omar: **mataa turiidu 'an nufarriqa haadhaa at-taqriir?** (*mah-tah too-ree-doo an noo-fah-ree-qah hah-zah ah-tak-reer?* When would you like to distribute this report?)

Samir: **'indanaa 'ijtimaa' fii saa'a. yajib 'an yakuun at-taqriir jaahiz li al-'ijtimaa'.** (*een-dah-nah eej-tee-mah fee sah-ah. yah-jeeb an yah-koon ah-tak-reer jah-heez lee al-eej-tee-mah.* We have a meeting in one hour. The report must be ready in time for the meeting.)

Omar: **sa yakuun jaahiz fii niSf saa'a. kam min nuskha yajib 'an naTba'?** (*Sah yah-koon jah-heez fee nee-sef sah-ah. kam meen noos-kah yah-jeeb an nat-bah?* It'll be ready in half an hour. How many copies do we need to print?)

Samir: **sa yakuun 'ashra mumathiliin fii al-'ijtimaa', wa laakin 'iTba' khamsat nuskhaat 'iDHaafiyya.** (*sah yah-koon ash-rah moo-mah-thee-leen fee al-eej-tee-mah, wah lah-keen eet-bah kam-sat noos-kat ee-dah-fee-yah.* There will be ten representatives at the meeting, but print five additional copies just in case.)

Omar: **fawran. hal hunaaka shay'un 'aakhar?** (*faw-ran. hal hoo-nah-kah shay-oon ah-kar?* Right away. Is there anything else?)

Samir: **na'am. 'i'lam kaatibatii min faDlik 'an ta'khudh mukaalamat al-haatifiyya li 'annanii sa 'akuun fii al-'ijtimaa'.** (*nah-am. eeh-lam kah-tee-bah-tee meen fad-leek an tah-kooz moo-kah-lah-mat al-hah-tee-fee-yah lee ah-nah-nee sah ah-koon fee al-eej-tee-mah.* Yes. Please inform my assistant to hold all my calls because I'll be at the meeting.)

Omar: **sa 'aquulu lihaa dhallika al-'aan.** (*sah ah-koo-loo lee-hah zah-lee-kah al-an.* I will tell her that right now.)

Words to Know

taqriir	tak-reer	report
taqriiraat	tak-ree-rat	reports
niSf	nee-sef	half
musaa'ada	moo-sah-ah-dah	help
ghurfa	ghoor-fah	room
'ijtimaa'	eej-tee-mah	meeting/ conference
Suwar	soo-war	pictures
bidaaya	bee-dah-yah	beginning
nihaaya	nee-hah-yah	ending
yaziid	yah-zeed	to add
farraqa	fah-rah-qah	distribute
jaahiz	jah-heez	ready (M)
jaahiza	jah-hee-zah	ready (F)

Taba'a	tah-bah-ah	to print
nuskhaat	noos-kat	copies
mumathil	moo-mah-theel	representative (M)
mumathila	moo-mah-thee-lah	representative (F)
mumathiliin	moo-mah-thee-leen	representatives (MP)
mumathilaat	moo-mah-thee-lat	representatives (FP)
'iDHaafiy	ee-zah-fee	additional (M)
'iDHaafiyya	ee-zah-fee-yah	additional (F)

Giving orders

The *imperative verb form,* also known as the *command form,* is used to give orders or directions. It's an important verb to know in the workplace because that's where you're usually told what to do and where you tell others what to do. The imperative structure is fairly straightforward. This section shares some quick tips to allow you to master the imperative form.

First, because the imperative is a command form, you can use it only with present personal pronouns such as **'anta** (*an-tah;* you) (M) and **'anti** (*an-tee;* you) (F). You can't use the imperative with absent personal pronouns such as **huwa** (*hoo-wah;* him) because you can't give an order to someone who isn't present. The following is a list of the personal pronouns to use with the imperative:

- ✔ **'anta** (*an-tah;* you) (MS)
- ✔ **'anti** (*an-tee;* you) (FS)
- ✔ **'antum** (*an-toom;* you) (MP)
- ✔ **'antunna** (*an-too-nah;* you) (FP)
- ✔ **'antumaa** (*an-too-mah;* you) (dual)

Second, the imperative form is nothing but a derived form of the regular verb in the **maaDii** (*mah-dee;* past) and the **MuDaari'** (*moo-dah-reeh;* present) tenses. The following is a list of the most common imperative verbs:

- ✔ **'uktub** (*ook-toob;* write)
- ✔ **'iqra** (*eek-rah;* read)
- ✔ **'unDHur** (*oon-zoor;* look)
- ✔ **'a'id** (*ah-eed;* repeat)
- ✔ **qull** (*kool;* say)
- ✔ **'u'kul** (*ooh-kool;* eat)
- ✔ **takallam** (*tah-kah-lam;* speak)
- ✔ **qif** (keef; stop)
- ✔ **taHarrak** (*tah-hah-rak;* move)

One of the more important verb command forms is the verb **kataba** (*kah-tah-bah;* to write). Table 8-1 shows the imperative (command) form of the verb **kataba**.

Table 8-1	Imperative Form of the Verb *kataba*		
Pronoun	*Imperative*	*Pronunciation*	*Translation*
'anta (you/MS)	'uktub	ook-toob	write (MS)
'anti (you/FS)	'uktubii	ook-too-bee	write (FS)
'antum (you/ MP)	'uktubuu	ook-too-boo	write (MP)
'antunna (you/ FP)	'uktubna	ook-toob-nah	write (FP)
'antumaa (dual)	'uktubaani	ook-too-bah-nee	write (dual)

Supplying your office

In order to function properly and efficiently at the **maktab,** you need a number of work-related items. Here are some supplies you can expect to find at the **maktab:**

- **kursiiy** (*koor-see;* chair)
- **maktab** (*mak-tab;* desk)
- **'aalat al-Hisaab** (*ah-lat al-hee-sab;* computer)
- **haatif** (*hah-teef;* telephone)
- **'aalat al-faks** (*ah-lat al-fah-kes;* fax machine)
- **maTba'a** (*mat-bah-ah;* printer)
- **'aalat al-Tibaa'** (*ah-lat ah-tee-bah;* photocopier)

Besides **'aalaat** (*ah-lat;* machines) and heavy furniture, you also need smaller tools:

- **qalam jaaf** (*qah-lam jaf;* pen)
- **qalam ar-rasaas** (*qah-lam ah-rah-sas;* pencil)
- **mimHaat** (*meem-hat;* eraser)
- **kitaab** (*kee-tab;* book)
- **daftar** (*daf-tar;* notebook)
- **'awraaq** (*aw-rak;* papers)
- **mishbak 'awraaq** (*meesh-bak aw-rak;* paper clip)
- **Dammat 'awraaq** (*dah-mat aw-rak;* stapler)
- **lisqah** (*lee-skah;* glue)
- **skooch** (*seh-koo-tech;* tape)

If you can't find a **daftar** or **lisqah,** ask a **zumalaa'** if you can borrow one. Here's how you ask a colleague a question, depending on whether you're speaking to a man or a woman:

✔ **hal 'indakii daftar?** (*hal een-dah-kee daf-tar;* Do you have a notebook?) (F)

✔ **hal 'indaka lisqah?** (*hal een-dah-kah lee-skah;* Do you have glue?) (M)

✔ **hal 'indakum skooch?** (*hal een-dah-koom seh-koo-tech;* Do you have tape?) (MP)

✔ **hal 'indahu qalam?** (*hal een-dah-hoo qah-lam;* Does he have a pen?)

Picking Up the Phone

The **haatif** (*haa-teef;* phone) is an important tool for the office. In this section, I explain how to properly begin and end a **mukaalama haatifiyya** (*moo-kaah-la-mah haa-teef-eeya;* phone conversation), how to make plans over the phone, and how to leave a proper phone message in Arabic.

Dialing up the basics

Before you can talk on the **haatif,** you need to be familiar with the following basic terminology:

✔ **haatif 'aam** (*haa-teef aahm;* public phone)

✔ **haatif selulayr** (*haa-teef seh-loo-layer;* cellphone)

✔ **raqm al-haatif** (*rak-em al-haa-teef;* phone number)

✔ **biTaaqat al-haatif** (*bee-taa-kaht al-haa-teef;* phone card)

✔ **mukaalama haatifiyya** (*moo-kaah-la-mah haa-teef-eeya;* phone conversation)

Beginning a phone conversation

You can begin a phone conversation in a number of ways. The most common, whether you're the caller or the person answering the phone, is to simply say **allo** (*all-low;* hello).

It's proper etiquette to state your name right after the person who picks up the phone says **allo,** particularly if you don't know that person. If you're the caller, you may say **'anaa** (*an-nah;* I am) followed by your name. Alternatively, you may say **haadhaa** (M) / **haadhihi** (F) (*haa-zaah / haa-zee-hee;* this is) followed by your name. A familiar phrase you can also use after you say **allo** is **'as-salaamu 'alaykum** (*ass-sa-laam-ou a-lai-koum;* hello) or **'ahlan wa sahlan** (*ahel-lan wah sahel-lan;* hi). Flip to Chapter 4 for more on greetings and making small talk.

Asking to speak to someone

Sometimes, a person other than the one you want to talk to answers the phone. A common phrase to help you ask for the person you called to speak with is

> **hal (insert name here) hunaa?** (*hal [name] hoo-naah*), which means "Is (name) here?"

Alternatively you can also use the personal pronouns **huwa** (if the person you're looking for is a man) or **hiya** (in the case of a woman) instead of using the person's name.

Making business appointments

If you need to set up a **maou'id** (*maw-oo-eed;* appointment) over the phone, the following conversation will give you some good phrases:

> Susan: **allo.** (*all-low.* Hello.)
>
> Katiba: **allo. sharikat rialto. daqiiqa min faDlik?** (*all-low. shah-ree-kaht ree-all-toh. dah-kee-qah meen fad-leek?* Hello. Rialto Inc. Can you wait one minute please?)
>
> Susan: **Tab'an.** (*tah-bah-'an.* Of course.)
>
> Katiba: **'afwan li-ta'akhur. kayfa 'usaa'iduk?** (*ah-feh-wan lee-tah-ah-khur. kay-fah oo-saa-ee-*

duk? Sorry to keep you waiting. How may I help you?)

Susan: **'uriidu 'an 'atakallam ma'a sayyid 'aHmad.** (*oo-ree-doo ann ah-tah-kah-llam ma-ah sah-yed ah-mad.* I would like to speak with Mr. Ahmed.)

Katiba: **sayyid 'aHmad mashghul. huwa fii 'ijtimaa'.** (*sah-yed ah-mad mash-ghool. hoo-wah fee eej-tee-maah.* Mr. Ahmed is busy. He is in a meeting.)

Susan: **mataa sa-yakun mawjood?** (*mah-taah sah-yah-koon maw-juud?* When will he be available?)

Katiba: **ayy daqiiqa.** (*ay dah-kee-qah.* Any minute now.)

Susan: **shukran jaziilan. sa-'ab-qaa fii al-khat.** (*shook-ran ja-zee-lan. sa-ah-bek-aah fee al-khah-t.* Thank you very much. I'll stay on the line.)

Words to Know

maou'id	maw-oo-eed	appointment
'ijtimaa'	eej-tee-maah	meeting
sayyid	say-yehd	Mr./Sir
sayyida	say-yee-dah	Mrs./Ms.
ra'iis	rah-ees	president
katiba	kah-tee-bah	secretary/assistant
sharika	shah-ree-kah	company
'usaa'iduk	oo-saa-ee-duk	help you
'uriidu	oo-ree-doo	would like
mashghul	mash-ghool	busy

Dealing with voice mail

When you leave a voice mail **khabaran** (*khah-bah-ran;* message) on someone's **haatif**, you want to make sure to include the following:

- ✔ Your **'ism** (*ee-seh-m;* name)

- ✔ The **waqt al-mukaalama** (*wah-ket al-muh-kaah-lah-mah;* time of the call)

- ✔ Your **raqm al-haatif** (*rah-kem al-haa-teef;* phone number or callback number)

- ✔ The **ahsan waqt li al-mukaalama** (*ah-sahn wah-ket lee al-muh-kaah-lah-mah;* best times you're available to talk)

A greeting message that you might hear on someone's phone could go like this:

> **'ahlan, haadhaa kareem. 'anaa lastu hunaa wa lakin 'idhaa takallamta 'ismuka wa raqamuka sa-'ukallimuk fii 'asra' waqt**

> *ahel-lan, hah-zah kah-reem. ah-nah las-too hoo-nah wah lah-keen ee-zah tah-kah-lam-tah ees-moo-kah wah rah-qah-moo-kah sah-oo-kah-lee-mook fee ass-rah wah-ket.*

> Hi, this is Karim. I'm not in right now, but if you leave your name and number, I'll get back to you as soon as possible.

Here's the message you might leave:

> **'ahlan wa sahlan karim. haadhihi selma. as-saa'a al-waaHida wa an-niSf yawm al-khamiis. khaabirnii min faDlik 'inda wuSuulika bi haadha al-khabar ba'ada as-saa'a al-khaamisa. raqmii Sifr waaHid ithnayn thalaatha. shukran!**

> *ahel-lan wah sahel-lan kah-reem. haa-zee-hee selma. ass-saa-ah al-waa-hee-dah wa-ann-nee-sef ya-woom al-kha-mees. khaa-bir-nee meen fahd-lik inn-dah wu-soo-li-kah bee haa-zaah al-khah-bar bah-dah as-saa-ah al-khaa-mee-sah. rak-mee see-fer waa-hid ith-nay-en tha-laah-thah. shook-ran!*

Hi Karim. This is Selma. It's 1:30 in the afternoon on Thursday. Please give me a call back when you get this message anytime after 5:00. My number is 0123. Thanks!

Chapter 9

I Get Around: Transportation

- -

In This Chapter
▶ Taking to the skies
▶ Catching taxis, buses, and trains
▶ Asking for directions

- -

*W*hen it comes to getting around the block, the city, or the world, you have a lot of different modes of **naql** (*nah-kel;* transportation) to choose from. In this chapter, I tell you not only how to use all major transportation methods but also how to navigate a Middle Eastern city and ask directions.

Traveling by Plane

One of the most common methods of **naql** is flying in a **Taa'ira** (*tah-ee-rah;* airplane). Chances are if you're in North America or Europe and want to go to the Middle East, you'll take a **Taa'ira.**

Making reservations

The first step in air travel is making a **Hajz** (*haj-z;* reservation) and buying a **biTaaqat as-safar** (*bee-tah-kaht ah-sah-far;* plane ticket). You may purchase your

biTaaqat as-safar by visiting your **wakiil safariyaat** (*wah-keel sah-fah-ree-yat;* travel agent) or by going online. The following conversation is one you might have with your travel agent:

Sophia: **'ahlan wa sahlan 'aHmed. haadhihi sofia.** (*ahel-an wah sa-hel-an ah-med. hah-zee-hee so-fee-ah.* Hi Ahmed. This is Sophia.)

Ahmed: **'ahlan sofia. kayfa yumkin 'an 'usaa'iduki?** (*ahel-an so-fee-ah. kay-fah yoom-keen ann oo-sah-ee-doo-kee?* Hi Sophia. How may I help you?)

Sophia: **'uriidu 'an 'adhhab 'ilaa 'ad-daar 'al-bayDaa' ma'a 'ummii li al-'uTla.** (*oo-ree-doo an az-hab ee-lah ah-dar al-bay-dah mah-ah oo-mee lee al-oot-lah.* I would like to go to Casablanca for the holidays with my mother.)

Ahmed: **raa'i'!** **haadhihi fikra mumtaaza. wa mataa turiidaani 'an tadhabaani?** (*rah-eeh! hah-zee-hee feek-rah moom-tah-zah. wah mah-tah too-ree-dah-nee an taz-hah-bah-nee?* Excellent! That's a great idea. And when would you like to go?)

Sophia: **nuriidu 'an nadhhab yawm as-sabt.** (*noo-ree-doo an naz-hab yah-oum ah-sabt.* We would like to go on Saturday.)

Ahmed: **kwayyis. ma'a 'ay saa'a?** (*kuh-wah-yees. mah-ah ay sah-ah?* Okay. At what time would you like to leave?)

Sophia: **hal 'indaka Tayaraan ma'a 'as-saa'a al-khaamisa?** (*hal een-dah-kah tay-yah-ran mah-ah ah-sah-ah al-kah-mee-sah?* Do you have any flights at 5:00?)

Ahmed: **na'am.** (*nah-am.* Yes.)

Sophia: **Tayyib. sana'khudh biTaaqatayn min faDlik.** (*tah-yeeb. sah-nah-kooz bee-tah-kah-tayn meen fad-leek.* Good. We'll take two tickets please.)

Ahmed: **hal turiidaani maqaa'id 'amaama 'an-naafida 'aw bayna al-maqaa'id?** (*hal too-ree-dah-nee mah-qah-eed ah-mah-mah ah-nah-fee-dah ah-ou bay-nah al-mah-qah-eed?* Would you like window or aisle seats?)

Sophia: **maqaa'id 'amaama 'an-naafida min faDlik.** (*mah-qah-eed ah-mah-mah ah-nah-fee-dah meen fad-leek.* Window seats please.)

Ahmed: **'indii biTaaqatayn li maqaa'id 'amaama 'an-naafida li Tayaarin li daar al-bayDaa' yawm as-sabt ma'a 'as-saa'a al-khaamisa.** (*een-dee bee-tah-kah-tayn lee mah-qah-eed ah-mah-mah ah-nah-fee-dah lee tah-yah-reen lee dar al-bay-dah ya-oum ah-sah-bet ma-ah ah-sah-ah al-kah-mee-sah.* So I have two tickets for window seats for a flight to Casablanca on Saturday at 5:00.)

Sophia: **mumtaaz!** (*moom-taz!* Excellent!)

Ahmed: **riHla sa'eeda!** (*reeh-lah sah-ee-dah!* Have a nice trip!)

Words to Know

'uTla	oot-lah	holiday/vacation
biTaaqa	bee-tah-kah	ticket
biTaaqatayn	bee-tah-kah-tayn	2 tickets
biTaaqaat	bee-tah-kaht	tickets (3 or more)
Tayaraan	tah-yah-ran	flight
maq'ad	mak-had	seat
maqaa'id	mah-qah-eed	seats (3 or more)
bayna al-maqaa'id	bay-nah al-mah-qah-eed	aisle seat(s)

continued

Words to Know (continued)

maq'ad an-naafida	mak-had ah-nah-fee-dah	window seat
riHla	reeh-lah	voyage
safar	sah-far	trip
musaafir	moo-sah-feer	traveler (M)
mussafira	moo-sah-fee-rah	traveler (F)
musaafiruun	moo-sah-fee-ruun	travelers (M)
musaafiraat	moo-sah-fee-rat	travelers (F)

Getting some legwork out of the verb "to travel"

If there's one verb you need to be familiar with relating to travel, it's the verb **saafara** (*sah-fah-rah*; to travel). Even though **saafara** has four consonants instead of the usual three, it's nevertheless considered to be a regular verb because the fourth consonant, the **'alif,** is actually a consonant that acts as a long vowel elongating the **siin.** (For more on regular verbs, flip to Chapter 2.)

Use the form **yusaafiru** to conjugate "traveling" in the present tense. Table 9-1 shows you how:

Table 9-1	The Present Tense of the Verb *saafara* (To Travel)	
Form	*Pronunciation*	*Translation*
'anaa 'usaafiru	*ah-nah oo-sah-fee-roo*	I am traveling

Form	Pronunciation	Translation
'anta tusaafiru	*ahn-tah too-sah-fee-roo*	You are traveling (MS)
'anti tusaafiriina	*ahn-tee too-sah-fee-ree-nah*	You are traveling (FS)
huwa yusaafiru	*hoo-wah yoo-sah-fee-roo*	He is traveling
hiya tusaafiru	*hee-yah too-sah-fee-roo*	She is traveling
naHnu nussafiru	*nah-noo noo-sah-fee-roo*	We are traveling
'antum tusaafiruuna	*ahn-toom too-sah-fee-roo-nah*	You are traveling (MP)
'antunna tusaafirna	*ahn-too-nah too-sah-feer-nah*	You are traveling (FP)
hum yusaafiruuna	*hoom yoo-sah-fee-roo-nah*	They are traveling (MP)
hunna yusaafirna	*hoo-nah yoo-sah-feer-nah*	They are traveling (FP)
antumaa tusaafiraani	*ahn-too-mah too-sah-fee-rah-nee*	You are traveling (dual/MP/FP)
humaa yusaafiraani	*hoo-mah yoo-sah-fee-rah-nee*	They are traveling (dual/MP)
humaa tusaafiraani	*hoo-mah too-sah-fee-rah-nee*	They are traveling (dual/FP)

Registering at the airport

With a **biTaaqat as-safar,** you're ready to head off to the **maTaar** (*mah-tar;* airport) and board the **Taa'ira.** But before you actually get on the **Taa'ira,** you need to take care of a few logistical things. First, you must present your **jawaaz as-safar** (*jah-waz ah-sah-far;* passport) and your **biTaaqat as-safar** at the airport **tasjiil** (*tass-jeel;* registration) desk, which is located in the **maHaTTat al-khuTuut al-jawwiya** (*mah-hah-tah al-koo-toot al-jah-wee-yah;* airport terminal).

Second, you must also answer some **'as'ila** (*ass-ee-lah;* questions) about your **safar** and your **'amti'a** (*am-tee-ah;* luggage):

- ✔ **kam min 'amti'a satusajjiliina?** (*kam meen am-tee-ah sah-too-sah-jee-lee-nah?* How many pieces of luggage are you going to register?)

- ✔ **hal naDHamti al-'amti'a binafsuki?** (*hal nah-zam-tee al-am-tee-ah bee-naf-soo-kee?* Did you pack your bags by yourself?)

- ✔ **hal kul shay' fii al-'amti'a milkuki?** (*hal kool shay fee al-am-tee-ah meel-koo-kee?* Is everything in the bags yours?)

- ✔ **hal kaanat al-'amti'a ma'akii fii kul al-waqt?** (*hal kah-nat al-am-tee-ah mah-ah-kee fee kool al-wah-ket?* Have you had the bags in your possession at all times?)

Words to Know

'amti'a	am-tee-ah	luggage
shanTa	shan-tah	suitcase
shanTatayn	shan-tah-tayn	two suitcases
miHfaDHa	meeh-fah-dah	briefcase
yusajjilu	yoo-sah-jee-loo	to register
naDHama	nah-zah-mah	to organize
ta'shiira	tah-shee-rah	visa
madkhal	mad-kal	gate

Boarding the plane

So you're ready to board the **Taa'ira!** After you check your **'amti'a** and present your **biTaaqat as-safar** and your **jawaaz as-safar** to the airline attendant, be sure to follow all **ta'liimaat** (*tah-lee-mat;* instructions) carefully.

When you reach the **madkhal** (*mad-kal;* gate) and board the **Taa'ira,** present your **biTaaqat as-safar** to the **muwaafiq aT-Taa'ira** (*moo-wah-feek ah-tah-ee-rah;* flight attendant), who will show you your **maq'ad** (*mak-had;* seat). The following terms are related to the **Taa'ira** and your flight:

- **raakib** (*rah-keeb;* passenger)
- **rukkaab** (*roo-kab;* passengers)
- **muwaafiq** (*moo-wah-feek;* attendant) (M)
- **muwaafiqa** (*moo-wah-fee-qah;* attendant) (F)
- **Tayyaar** (*tah-yar;* pilot) (M)
- **Tayyaara** (*tah-yah-rah;* pilot) (F)
- **ghurfat al-qiyaada** (*ghoor-fat al-kee-yah-dah;* cockpit)
- **mirHaad** (*meer-had;* bathroom)
- **mirHaad mashghuul** (*meer-had mash-ghool;* bathroom occupied)
- **'araba fii 'a'laa** (*ah-rah-bah fee ah-lah;* overhead compartment)
- **qism al-'awwal** (*kee-sem al-ah-wal;* first class)
- **qism al-'a'maal** (*kee-sem al-ah-mal;* business class)
- **qism 'iqtiSaadii** (*kee-sem eek-tee-sah-dee;* "economy" class)
- **sur'a** (*soor-ah;* speed)
- **'irtifaa'** (*eer-tee-fah;* altitude)
- **'inTilaaq** (*een-tee-lak;* departure)
- **wuSuul** (*woo-sool;* arrival)

A brief departure on the verb "to arrive"

A helpful verb to know when you're traveling is **waSala** (*wah-sah-lah;* to arrive). (You can also use the verb **waSala** to express "to land" or "to come.") Even though **waSala** has three consonants and therefore should fall into the mold of regular verb forms, it's nevertheless classified as an irregular verb because it includes the initial consonant **waaw.** Verbs with initial **waaw** are classified as irregular because their present tense forms are different than the regular present tense verb forms. As a result, whereas the past tense of **waSala** follows a regular pattern, the present does not. You need to use the irregular form **yaSilu** to conjugate "arriving" in the present tense. Table 9-2 shows you how:

Table 9-2	The Present Tense of the Verb *waSala* (To Arrive)	
Form	*Pronunciation*	*Translation*
'anaa 'aSilu	*ah-nah ah-see-loo*	I am arriving
'anta taSilu	*ahn-tah tah-see-loo*	You are arriv-ing (MS)
'anti taSiliina	*ahn-tee tah-see-lee-nah*	You are arriv-ing (FS)
huwa yaSilu	*hoo-wah yah-see-loo*	He is arriving
hiya taSilu	*hee-yah tah-see-loo*	She is arriving
naHnu naSilu	*nah-noo nah-see-loo*	We are arriving
'antum taSiluuna	*ahn-toom tah-see-loo-nah*	You are arriv-ing (MP)
'antunna taSilna	*ahn-too-nah tah-seel-nah*	You are arriv-ing (FP)

Form	Pronunciation	Translation
hum yaSiluuna	*hoom yah-see-loo-nah*	They are arriving (MP)
hunna yaSilna	*hoo-nah yah-seel-nah*	They are arriving (FP)
antumaa taSilaani	*ahn-too-mah tah-see-lah-nee*	You are arriving (dual/MP/FP)
humaa yaSilaani	*hoo-mah yah-see-lah-nee*	They are arriving (dual/MP)
humaa taSilaani	*hoo-mah tah-see-lah-nee*	They are arriving (dual/FP)

Going through immigration and customs

When your **Taa'ira** lands and you arrive at your chosen destination, it's time to deal with the **hijra** (*heej-rah;* immigration) and **diwaana** (*dee-wah-nah;* customs) officials. In recent years, airports have established more stringent requirements on **musaafiruun** (*moo-sah-fee-ruun;* travelers), so be prepared to answer a number of **'as'ila** regarding the details and purpose of your **safar.** Here are some common questions a **hijra** or **diwaana** official may ask you:

- ✔ **maa 'ismuk?** (*mah ees-mook;* What's your name?)

- ✔ **kam 'umruk?** (*kam um-rook;* How old are you?)

- ✔ **'ayna taskun?** (*eh-yeh-nah tass-koon;* Where do you live?)

- ✔ **maa hiya mihnatuk?** (*mah hee-yah meeh-nah-took;* What do you do?)

- ✔ **kam muddat safaruk?** (*kam moo-dat sah-fah-rook;* How long is your trip?)

- ✔ **maa hadaf safaruk?** (*mah hah-daf sah-fah-rook;* What's the purpose of your trip?)

- **'ayna sataskun li muddat as-safar?** (*eh-yeh-nah sah-tass-koon lee moo-dat ah-sah-far;* Where will you be staying during the trip?)

- **hal tusaafir biwaHdik?** (*hal too-sah-feer bee-wah-deek;* Are you traveling alone?)

Provide clear and accurate answers to these questions. Providing false statements to an official from **hijra** or **diwaana** is a serious offense, so make sure you're truthful throughout the questioning.

If you're visiting a Muslim country, check with your travel agent or consular official about restrictions certain countries may have regarding bringing particular items into the country. For example, if you're traveling to Saudi Arabia, you can't bring alcohol with you into the country; and if you're a woman, you may have to wear specific clothing, such as the **Hijaab** (*hee-jab;* veil), in order to comply with local religious laws. You want to be certain you are aware of all the rules and laws before you face someone from **hijra** or **diwaana**.

Words to Know

jinsiyya	jeen-see-yah	nationality
sanat al-miilaad	sah-nat al-mee-lad	date of birth
'iid al-miilaad	eed al-mee-lad	birthday
hadaf	hah-daf	purpose/goal
taariikh	tah-reek	date
khuruuj	koo-rooj	exit/departure

dukhuul	doo-kool	entry
siyaaHa	see-yah-hah	tourism
saa'iH	sah-eeh	tourist (M)
saa'iHa	sah-ee-hah	tourist (F)
muhaajir	moo-hah-jeer	immigrant (M)
muhaajira	moo-hah-jee-rah	immigrant (F)
muhaajiruun	moo-hah-jee-roon	immigrants (M)
muhaajiraat	moo-hah-jee-rat	immigrants (F)

Getting through the **hijra** post puts you one step closer to leaving the **maTaar** and discovering the wonders of the exotic country you're visiting! After your interview with the **hijra,** you may proceed to pick up your **'amti'a.** You may use the help of a **Hammaal** (*hah-mal;* baggage handler/porter), or you may simply use an **'ariiba** (*ah-ree-bah;* cart) to haul your own luggage.

Before you actually leave the **maTaar,** you must go through **diwaana** (customs). Use the following phrases when speaking with **diwaana** officials:

- ✔ **laa shay' li al-'i'laan.** (*lah shay lee al-eeh-lan;* Nothing to declare.)
- ✔ **'indii shay' li al-'i'laan.** (*een-dee shay lee al-eeh-lan;* I have something to declare.)

Getting Around on Land

Major metropolitan areas and most small towns have a number of transportation methods you can choose from. Table 9-3 lists some of the most common forms of transportation you're likely to use.

Table 9-3	Major Forms of Transportation	
Arabic	*Pronunciation*	*Translation*
Taaksii	tak-see	taxi
Haafila	hah-fee-lah	bus
qiTaar	kee-tar	train
nafaq 'arDiiy	nah-fak ar-dee	subway
safiina	sah-fee-nah	ship
Sayyaara	sah-yah-rah	car
Sayyaara 'ijaariya	sah-yah-rah ee-jah-ree-yah	rental car
darraaja	dah-rah-jah	bicycle
darraaja naariyya	dah-rah-jah nah-ree-yah	motorcycle

Hailing a taxi

When hailing a cab in a foreign country, keep the following advice in mind:

✔ **Make sure that the taxi you hail is fully licensed and authorized by the local agencies to operate as a taxi.** A number of companies operate illegal taxis and take advantage of unsuspecting tourists — make sure you're not one of them! Most legitimate taxi operators have licensing information on display somewhere inside the cab or even on the car's exterior.

✔ **Be aware that most taxis that run to and from the airport charge a flat rate.** Inquire about the flat rate before you get into the taxi.

✔ **If you're in the city, make sure the taxi saa'iq** (*sah-eek;* driver) **turns on the Hasuub** (*hah-soob;* meter). A common occurrence is that a driver forgets (either accidentally or intentionally) to turn on the meter and ends up charging you an exorbitant amount of money for a short ride.

In most Arab and Middle Eastern countries, tipping the **saa'iq** is not required. However, I'm sure the **saa'iq** won't argue if you decide to give him a little tip!

Words to Know

'iHtafiDH	eeh-tah-feed	keep (command form)
baaqii	bah-kee	change (money)
thaman tadhkiira	tah-man taz-kee-rah	fare
Hasuub	hah-soob	counter/meter

Taking a bus

The **Haafila** (*hah-fee-lah;* bus) is a convenient mode of transportation whether you're traveling across town or across the country. If you're in a city and traveling within city limits, taking the bus is a good option because it usually costs less than a taxi. If you're traveling across the country, not only is taking a bus an economical option, but you also get to enjoy the beautiful scenery!

Most **Haafilaat** (*hah-fee-lat;* buses) accept prepaid **biTaaqaat** (*bee-tah-kaht;* tickets). If you take the **Haafila** frequently, refill your **biTaaqa** regularly. Otherwise, if you take a bus only occasionally, you'll be glad to know that most **Haafilaat** also accept **fuluus** (*foo-loos;* cash) as long as it's small bills. Here are some common terms you may need or encounter if you decide to take a **Haafila:**

- ✔ **biTaaqat al-Haafila** (*bee-tah-kaht al-hah-fee-lah;* bus ticket)

- ✔ **maHaTTat al-Haafila** (*mah-hah-tat al-hah-fee-lah;* bus station/bus stop)

- ✔ **saa'iq al-Haafila** (*sah-eek al-hah-fee-lah;* bus driver)

- ✔ **tawqiit al-Haafila** (*taw-keet al-hah-fee-lah;* bus schedule)

If you want to say "every" as in "every day" or "every hour," all you do is add the word **kul** (*kool;* every) before the noun that describes the time you're referring to. For example:

- ✔ **kul yawm** (*kool yawm;* every day)

- ✔ **kul saa'a** (*kool sah-ah;* every hour)

- ✔ **kul niSf saa'a** (*kool nee-sef sah-ah;* every half hour)

- ✔ **kul rubu' saa'a** (*kool roo-booh sah-ah;* every 15 minutes)

Here are some other phrases to help you find the bus you need:

- ✔ **'afwan, hal haadhihi al-Haafila tadhhab 'ilaa waSat al-madiina?** (*af-wan, hal hah-zee-hee al-hah-fee-lah taz-hab ee-lah wah-sat al-mah-dee-nah?* Excuse me, does this bus go downtown?)

- ✔ **'ayna al-Haafila 'ilaa waSat al-madiina?** (*eh-yeh-nah al-hah-fee-lah ee-lah wah-sat al-mah-dee-nah?* Which bus goes downtown?)

- ✔ **mataa sataSil al-Haafila raqm 'ashra?** (*mah-tah sah-tah-sil al-hah-fee-lah rah-kem ash-rah?* When does bus number 10 arrive?)

Boarding a train

The **qiTaar** (*kee-tar;* train) is a popular alternative if you're looking for transportation that's convenient, fast, affordable, and allows you to do a little sight-seeing while you're on the go. When you board the **qiTaar,** be ready to provide your **biTaaqa** to the **qiTaar** attendant. Although boarding most **qiTaar** doesn't require a **biTaaqa shakhSiyya** (*bee-tah-kah shak-see-yah;* personal ID card), you should be ready to present one if an attendant asks you for it.

Asking for Directions

Being able to ask for — and understand — **'ittijaahaat**
(*ee-tee-jah-hat;* directions) is an important skill. In this
section, I tell you how to interact with native speakers
in order to get relevant information to help you find
what you're looking for!

Asking "where" questions

The best way to get directions-related information
from Arabic speakers is to ask **'ayna** (*eh-yeh-nah;*
where) questions. Luckily, the structure of an **'ayna**
question is relatively straightforward: You use **'ayna**
followed by the subject. For example:

- ✔ **'ayna al-funduq?** (*eh-yeh-nah al-foon-dook;*
  Where is the hotel?)

- ✔ **'ayna al-haatif?** (*eh-yeh-nah al-haa-teef;* Where is
  the phone?)

- ✔ **'ayna al-mirHaaD?** (*eh-yeh-nah al-meer-haad;*
  Where is the bathroom?)

Be sure to define the subject following **'ayna.**
You define a subject by adding the definite
article prefix **al-** to the subject noun. For
example, **funduq** means "hotel," and **al-funduq** means "the hotel." So if you're asking
where the hotel is located, you say, **'ayna al-
funduq?** (Where is the hotel?) and not **'ayna
funduq?,** which translates to "Where is
hotel?"

Answering "where" questions

You can answer an **'ayna** question in a number of
different ways, ranging from the simple to the convo-
luted. In order to answer **'ayna** questions, you have to
understand the structure of the **'ayna** question reply,
which usually follows this format: subject, preposition, object.

Take a look at some common **'ayna** questions and their corresponding replies:

- **'ayna al-mustashfaa?** (*eh-yeh-nah al-moos-tash-faah;* Where is the hospital?)

  al-mustashfaa fii al-madiina. (*al-moos-tash-faah fee al-mah-dee-nah;* The hospital is in the city.)

- **'ayna al-maT'am?** (*eh-yeh-nah al-mah-tam;* Where is the restaurant?)

  al-maT'am qariib min al-funduq. (*al-mah-tam qah-reeb meen al-foon-dook;* The restaurant is close to the hotel.)

- **'ayna al-kitaab?** (*eh-yeh-nah al-kee-taab;* Where is the book?)

  al-kitaab taHta aT-Taawila. (*al-kee-taab tah-tah at-tah-wee-lah;* The book is underneath the table.)

Notice that in these examples, you use a preposition to establish a connection between the subject (in this case, what or who you're looking for) and the object (the location of the desired subject). In order to establish the desired relationship, it's very important for you to be familiar with some common prepositions:

- **'alaa** (*ah-laah;* on)
- **fii** (*fee;* in)
- **'ilaa** (*ee-laah;* to)
- **qariib min** (*qah-reeb meen;* close to)
- **ba'id min** (*bah-eed meen;* far from)
- **bijaanib** (*bee-jaah-neeb;* next to)
- **fawqa** (*faw-qah;* on top of)
- **taHta** (*tah-tah;* underneath/below)
- **'amaama** (*ah-maah-mah;* in front of)
- **waraa'a** (*wah-raah-ah;* behind)
- **yamiin min** (*yah-meen meen;* right of)
- **yasiir min** (*yah-seer meen;* left of)

The subject in the reply to an **'ayna** question must also be defined. In addition, the object in the **'ayna** reply statement should be defined as well, either by using the definite article prefix **al-** or by including a predefined object.

Asking with courtesy

Of course, you can't just go up to someone and ask them bluntly, **'ayna al-funduq?** (Where is the hotel?). That wouldn't be very polite. The proper etiquette for approaching someone and asking for directions is to first say **as-salaamu 'alaykum** (*ah-sah-lah-moo ah-lay-koom;* hello) or **'ahlan wa sahlan** (*ah-hel-an wah sah-hel-an;* hi) and then ask if he or she would permit you to ask a question. For example, you begin the exchange by saying:

> **'afwan. hal yumkin 'an 'as'alaka su'aal?** (*ahf-wan. Hal yoom-keen an ass-ah-lah-kah soo-aah-l;* Excuse me. May I ask you a question?)

After the person agrees to take your question, you may proceed to ask for directions.

Could you repeat that?

Sometimes, when you ask for directions, the person who tries to help you starts talking too fast and you can't quite understand what he or she is saying. Other times, you may be in a loud area, such as near a down-town traffic jam, and you can't make out what the other person is saying. In either case, you have to ask the person who's giving you directions to speak more slowly or to repeat what he or she has just said. These phrases can help you cope with these situations:

✔ **'afwan** (*ahf-wan;* excuse me/pardon me)

✔ **'ismaH lii** (*ees-maah lee;* excuse me)

✔ **laa 'afham** (*laa ah-fham;* I don't understand)

✔ **takallam bi baT'in min faDlik** (*tah-kah-lahm bee bat-een meen fahd-leek;* speak slowly please)

✔ **hal yumkin 'an ta'id min faDlik?** (*hal yoom-keen an tah-eed meen fahd-leek;* Could you repeat please?)

✔ **'a'id min faDlik** (*ah-eed meen fahd-leek;* Repeat please)

✔ **maadhaa qult?** (*maah-zaah koo-let;* What did you say?)

Here's a conversation that puts these phrases to use:

John: **'afwan. hal yumkin 'an 'as'alaka su'aal?** (*ahf-wan. hal yoom-keen an ass-ah-lah-kah soo-aah-l? Excuse me. May I ask you a question?*)

Maria: **na'am.** (*nah-ahm. Yes.*)

John: **'ayna al-madrasa?** (*eh-yeh-nah al-mah-drah-sah? Where is the school?*)

Maria: **maa 'ismu al-madrasa?** (*maah ees-muh al-mah-drah-sah? What's the name of the school?*)

John: **al-madrasa al-amriikiiyya.** (*al-mah-drah-sah al-am-ree-kee-yah. The American school.*)

Maria: **al-madrasa ba'iida min hunaa.** (*al-mah-drah-sah bah-ee-dah meen hoo-naah. The school is far from here.*)

John: **laa 'afham. hal yumkin 'an ta'id min faDlik?** (*laa ah-fham. hal yoom-keen an tah-eed meen fahd-leek? I don't understand. Could you repeat please?*)

Maria: **al-madrasa laysat qariiba min hunaa. yajib 'an ta'khudh al-haafila 'ilaa waSat al-madiina.** (*al-mah-drah-sah lay-saht qah-ree-bah meen hoo-naah. yah-jeeb an tah-khoo-dh al-haa-fee-lah ee-laah wah-saht al-mah-dee-nah. The school is not close to here. You must take the bus to the center of the city.*)

John: **fahamt! Shukran jaziilan.** (*fah-ha-met! shook-ran jah-zee-lan. I understand! Thank you very much.*)

Maria: **'afwan.** (*ahf-wan. You're welcome.*)

Words to Know

ba'iid	bah-eed	far (M)
ba'iida	bah-eed-ah	far (F)
qariib	qah-reeb	close (M)
qariiba	qah-reeb-ah	close (F)
hunaa	hoo-naah	here
hunaaka	hoo-naah-kah	there
'afham	ahf-ham	understand
haafila	haa-fee-lah	bus
taksii	tak-see	taxi
qitaar	kee-tar	train
maHaTTa	mah-hah-tah	station

Using command forms

When you ask someone for directions, the person directs you to a specific location. Essentially, he or she tells you where to go, which qualifies as a *command form*. The command form applies to all personal pronouns, but you have to use different commands for men and women. Here are some common command forms:

Masculine Command	*Feminine Command*
'a'id (*ah-eed;* repeat)	**'a'idii** (*ah-eed-ee;* repeat)
'idhhab (*eez-hab;* go)	**'idhhabii** (*eez-hab-ee;* go)
khudh (*khooz;* take)	**khudhii** (*khooz-ee;* take)

(continued)

(continued)

Masculine Command	Feminine Command
Tuf (*toof;* turn)	**Tufii** (*toof-ee;* turn)
qif (*keef;* stop)	**qifii** (*keef-ee;* stop)

Note: '**imshii** (*eem-shee;* walk) is a special command form that is gender-neutral.

The following conversation shows how the command form is used to tell someone how to get to their destination:

Susan: **'afwan. hal yumkin 'an 'as'alaka su'aal?** (*ahf-wan. hal yoom-keen an ass-ah-lah-kah soo-aah-l?* Excuse me. May I ask you a question?)

Rita: **Taba'an.** (*tah-bah-an.* Of course.)

Susan: **'ayna funduq al-jawhara?** (*eh-yeh-nah foon-dook al-jaw-ha-rah?* Where is the Jawhara Hotel?)

Rita: **'aDHunnu 'anna haadhaa al-funduq fii waSat al-madiina.** (*ah-zuh-nuh an-nah hah-zah al-foon-dook fee wah-sat al-mah-dee-nah.* I believe that this hotel is in the center of the city.)

Susan: **na'am. kayfa 'adhhabu hunaaka?** (*nah-ahm. kay-fah az-hah-boo hoo-nah-kah?* Yes. How do I get there?)

Rita: **Taba'an. 'idhhabii 'ilaa shaari' Hassan thumma Tufii 'ilaa al-yamiin.** (*tah-bah-an. eez-hab-ee ee-laah shah-reeh hah-san thoo-mah toof-ee ee-laah al-yah-meen.* Certainly. Go to Avenue Hassan, then turn right.)

Susan: **kwayyis.** (*kwah-yees.* Okay.)

Rita: **thumma 'imshii 'ilaa al-maktaba wa qifii. al-funduq 'amaama al-maktaba. Al-funduq fii ash-shamaal.** (*thoo-maah eem-shee ee-laah al-mak-tah-bah wah keef-ee. al-foon-dook ah-maah-mah al-mak-tah-bah. al-foon-dook fee as-shah-maal.* Then walk toward the library and stop. The hotel is in front of the library. The hotel is facing north.)

Susan: **shukran li musaa'adatuki.** (*shook-ran lee moo-saa-ah-dah-too-kee.* Thank you for your help.)

Words to Know

'aDHunnu	ah-zuh-nnuh	I believe
Thumma	thoo-mah	then
kwayyis	kwah-yees	okay
musaa'ada	moo-saa-ah-dah	help
shamaal	shah-maal	north
janoub	jah-noob	south
sharq	shah-rek	east
gharb	ghah-reb	west

Chapter 10

Laying Down Your Weary Head: Hotel or Home

- -

In This Chapter

▶ Hunting for the right accommodation

▶ Reserving your room

▶ Checking in and out

▶ Making a home

- -

*P*icking the right **funduq** (*foon-dook;* hotel) for you and your family or friends can sometimes make or break your **safar** (*sah-far;* trip). During a **safar** or **riHla** (*reeh-lah;* vacation), the **funduq** is your home away from home.

In this chapter, I show you the ins and outs of choosing the right **funduq** to meet your travel, budgetary, and personal needs. You find out how to inquire about specific aspects of the **funduq** (such as available amenities and proximity to the city center), how to make a room reservation and check into your room, how to interact with the **funduq** staff, and, last but not least, how to successfully check out of your hotel room!

If you're staying in someone's home (or establishing your own), I also offer some key terms to help you navigate around the house.

Choosing the Right Accommodation

When choosing the right **funduq,** you need to consider a number of factors:

- **thaman** (*tah-man;* price)
- **ghurfa** (*ghoor-fah;* room)
- **Hajem al-ghurfa** (*hah-jem al-ghoor-fah;* room size)
- **naw' al-ghurfa** (*nah-ouh al-ghoor-fah;* room type)
- **khidmat al-ghurfa** (*keed-mat al-ghoor-fah;* room service)
- **'iiwaa'** (*ee-wah;* accommodations)
- **maraafiq** (*mah-rah-feek;* amenities)
- **masbaH** (*mas-bah;* swimming pool)
- **maT'am** (*mat-ham;* restaurant)

When inquiring about a **ghurfa,** you may need to use the following terms:

- **ghurfa li-shakhS waaHid** (*ghoor-fah lee-sha-kes wah-heed;* single room)
- **ghurfa li-shakhsayn** (*ghoor-fah lee-shak-sayn;* double room)
- **sariir** (*sah-reer;* bed)
- **mirHaad** (*meer-had;* toilet)
- **balcoon** (*bal-koon;* balcony)
- **tilifizyoon** (*tee-lee-feez-yoon;* television)
- **Tabaq** (*tah-bak;* floor/level)

To create a possessive noun in English, you usually use an apostrophe, such as "the girl's cat" or "the woman's house." It's the same in Arabic, except that you reverse the word order — you use an indefinite noun followed by a definite noun, as in **Hajem al-ghurfa. al-ghurfa** (a definite noun because it contains the definite article prefix **al-**) means "the room," and **Hajem** (an indefinite noun) means "size." So when you read or hear **Hajem al-ghurfa,** you automatically know that the **ghurfa** is the possessor acting on the **Hajem** (size) to express the "room's size" or, literally, "the size of the room."

Here are some other phrases that may come in handy:

- ✔ **'uriidu 'an 'a'raf 'idhaa kaana 'indakum ghuraf faarigha.** (*oo-ree-doo ann ah-raf ee-zah kah-nah een-dah-koom ghoo-raf fah-ree-ghah.* I would like to know whether you have any rooms available.)

- ✔ **hal 'indakum ghuraf li-shakhsayn?** (*hal een-dah-koom ghoo-raf lee-shak-sayn?* Do you have any double rooms?)

- ✔ **hal fii al-Hammaam duush wa banyoo?** (*hal fee al-hah-mam doosh wah ban-yoo?* Is there a shower and a bathtub in the bathroom?)

- ✔ **hal fii al-ghurfa khizaana?** (*hal fee al-ghoor-fah kee-zah-nah?* Is there a safe in the room?)

- ✔ **hal al-ghurfa 'indahaa mikwaa al-malaabis?** (*hal al-ghoor-fah een-dah-hah meek-wah al-mah-lah-bees?* Does the room come equipped with a clothes iron?)

- ✔ **kam min sariir fii haadhihi al-ghurfa?** (*kam meen sah-reer fee hah-zee-hee al-ghoor-fah?* How many beds are in this room?)

- ✔ **hal 'indahaa balcoon?** (*hal een-dah-hah bal-koon?* Does it have a balcony?)

- ✔ **sa-a'khudh haadhihi al-ghurfa.** (*sah-ah-kooz hah-zee-hee al-ghoor-fah.* I'll take this room.)

Words to Know

ghuraf	ghoo-raf	rooms
faarigha	fah-ree-ghah	available
naafida	nah-fee-dah	window
Hammaam	hah-mam	bathroom
duush	doosh	shower
banyoo	ban-yoo	bathtub
maghsala	mag-sah-lah	sink
fuuTa	foo-tah	towel
mir'aat	meer-at	mirror
wisaada	wee-sah-dah	pillow
baTTaniyya	bah-tah-nee-yah	blanket
miSbaaH	mees-bah	lamp
haatif	hah-teef	phone
midyaa'	meed-yah	radio
khizaana	kee-zah-nah	safe deposit box
mushrifat al-ghurfa	moosh-ree-fat al-ghoor-fah	room staff attendant

Making a Reservation

After you identify the right **funduq** with the right **maraafiq** and **ghurfa,** you're ready to make a **Hajzu** (*haj-zoo;* reservation). Before you do, though, you have a few considerations to make, such as the duration and length of your stay, the number and type of **ghuraf** you're reserving, the number of people staying, and the cost to stay at the **funduq**. This section explores all these elements so that you can be prepared to make a smooth **Hajzu** and secure the best accommodation for your **safar!**

Figuring out the price

thaman (*tah-man;* price) is an important factor to think about before you make your **Hajzu**. Fortunately, there are many accommodation options to suit every **mizaaniya** (*mee-zah-nee-yah;* budget). If you can afford it, making a **Hajzu** in a **funduq faakhir** (*foon-dook fah-kheer;* luxury hotel) is nice. If you're a **Taalib** (*tah-leeb;* student), staying at a **daar aT-Talaba** (*dar ah-tah-lah-bah;* youth hostel) is a more affordable option.

When making your **Hajzu,** be sure to inquire about any special **tanziilaat** (*tan-zee-lat;* discounts) that the **funduq** might be offering. Here are some **tanziilaat** you can ask about:

- ✔ **tanziilaat al-majmoo'aat** (*tan-zee-lat al-maj-moo-at;* group discounts)

- ✔ **tanziilaat as-saa'aat baTaala** (*tan-zee-lat ah-sah-at bah-tah-lah;* off-peak discounts)

- ✔ **tanziilaat al-fuSul** (*tan-zee-lat al-foo-sool;* seasonal discounts)

- ✔ **rayTaat as-safar** (*ray-tat ah-sah-far;* special travel packages)

And here are some of the questions you'll need to ask to take advantage of these discounts:

- ✔ **kam thaman ghurfa li-shakhS waaHid li muddat layla waaHida?** (*kam tah-man ghoor-fah lee-sha-kes wah-heed lee moo-dat lay-lah wah-hee-dah?* How much is a single room for one night?)

- ✔ **hal 'indakum 'ay tanziilaat li al-fuSul?** (*hal een-dah-koom ay tan-zee-lat lee al-foo-sool?* Do you have any seasonal discounts?)

Indicating the length of your stay

Making sure you get the room you want when you need it is as important as sticking to your **funduq** budget. Securing a **ghurfa** can be difficult, particularly during the **faSl al-'uTla** (*fah-sel al-oot-lah;* holiday season); therefore, it's advisable you make your **Hajzu** ahead of schedule so that you're assured to get the **ghurfa** you want during the **mudda** (*moo-dah;* period) of your choosing.

To say you're going to stay at the **funduq** "for a period of" so much time, use the following formula: **li muddat** (*lee moo-dat*) followed by the duration of your stay. For example, to say you're staying "for a period of a week," say **li muddat 'usbuu'** (*lee moo-dat oos-booh*). Here are some other examples:

- ✔ **li muddat yawm** (*lee moo-dat yah-oum;* for a period of one day)

- ✔ **li muddat khamsat 'ayyam** (*lee moo-dat kam-sat ah-yam;* for a period of five days)

- ✔ **li muddat 'usbuu' wa niSf** (*lee moo-dat oos-booh wah nee-sef;* for a period of one and a half weeks)

To say that you're staying from one date until another date, use the prepositions **min** (*meen;* from) and **'ilaa** (*ee-lah;* until). For example, if you're staying "from Monday until Thursday," you say **min al-'ithnayn 'ilaa al-khamiis** (*meen al-eeth-nayn ee-lah al-kah-mees*). Here are some other examples:

- ✔ **min al-'arbi'aa' 'ilaa al-'aHad** (*meen al-ar-bee-ah ee-lah al-ah-had;* from Thursday until Sunday)

- ✔ **min 'ishriin yulyuu 'ilaa thalaathiin yulyuu** (*meen eesh-reen yoo-leh-yoo ee-lah thah-lah-theen yoo-leh-yoo;* from July 20 until July 30)

- ✔ **min 'aghusTus 'ilaa sibtambar** (*meen ah-ghoo-seh-toos ee-lah seeb-tam-bar;* from August until September)

- ✔ **'uriidu haadhihi al-ghurfa li-muddat 'usbuu'.** (*oo-ree-doo hah-zee-hee al-ghoor-fah lee-moo-dat* *oos-booh.* I'd like this room for a period of one week.)

✔ **'uriidu haadhihi al-ghurfa min Disambar al-'awwal 'ilaa Disambar as-saabi'.** (*oo-ree-doo hah-zee-hee al-ghoor-fah meen dee-sahm-bar al-ah-wal ee-lah dee-sahm-bar ah-sah-bee.* I'd like this room from December 1 until December 7.)

And if you do want to take a vacation during the holidays, you can ask

hal haadhihi al-ghurfa mawjuuda li 'uTlat nihaayat as-sana? (*hal hah-zee-hee al-ghoor-fah maw-joo-dah lee oot-lat nee-hah-yat ah-sah-nah?* Is this room available during the end of year holiday?)

The verb for "to stay" is **baqaa** in the past tense and **yabqaa** in the present. To put a **fi'l** (*fee-ehl;* verb) in the **mustaqbal** (*moos-tak-bal;* future), all you do is add the prefix **sa-** to the **fi'l** in the present tense. For example, to communicate "I will stay for a period of one week," you say **sa-'abqaa li muddat 'usbuu'** (*sah-ab-qah lee moo-dat oos-booh*).

Checking In to the Hotel

When you arrive at your **funduq** after a long **safar,** probably the last thing on your mind is going through the formalities of checking in. If you already have a **Hajzu,** ask the **muwaDHaf al-'istiqbaal** (*moo-wah-daf al-ees-teek-bal;* desk clerk) for more **ma'luumaat** (*mah-loo-mat;* information). You might try this phrase:

'ahlan. 'indii Hajzu li ghurfa li-shakhs waaHid li muddat 'usbuu' bidaa'an al-yawm. (*ah-lan. een-dee haj-zoo lee ghoor-fah lee-shah-kes wah-heed lee moo-dat oos-booh bee-dah-an al-yah-oum.* Hi. I have a reservation for a single room for one week beginning today.)

If you don't have a **Hajzu,** you can inquire about room **mawjooda** (*maw-joo-dah;* availability) at the front desk. Here are some important terms you may need during check-in:

- **miftaH** (*meef-tah;* key)

- **miftaH al-ghurfa** (*meef-tah al-ghoor-fah;* room key)

- **'amti'a** (*am-tee-ah;* luggage)

- **shanTa** (*shan-tah;* suitcase)

- **miHfaDHa** (*meeh-fah-dah;* briefcase)

- **Tabiq** (*tah-beek;* floor)

- **miS'ad** (*mees-ad;* elevator)

- **'istiqbaal** (*ees-teek-bal;* reception)

- **maktab al-'istiqbaal** (*mak-tab al-ees-teek-bal;* reception desk)

- **muwaDHaf al-'istiqbaal** (*moo-wah-daf al-ees-teek-bal;* desk clerk) (M)

- **muwaDHafa al-'istiqbaal** (*moo-wah-dah-fah al-ees-teek-bal;* desk clerk) (F)

- **bawwaab** (*bah-wab;* concierge) (M)

- **bawwaaba** (*bah-wah-bah;* concierge) (F)

- **maDmuun** (*mad-moon;* included)

When interacting with the **funduq** staff, the following key phrases are likely to come in handy:

- **hal al-fuTuur maDmuun ma'a al-ghurfa?** (*hal al-foo-toor mad-moon mah-ah al-ghoor-fah;* Is breakfast included with the room?)

- **mataa yabda'u al-fuTuur?** (*mah-tah yab-dah-oo al-foo-toor;* When does breakfast begin?)

- **mataa yantahii al-fuTuur?** (*mah-tah yan-tah-hee al-foo-toor;* When does breakfast end?)

- **hal hunaaka khabaran lii?** (*hal hoo-nah-kah kah-bah-ran lee;* Are there any messages for me?)

✔ **'uriidu nahaad bi shakel mukaalama ma'a as-saa'a as-saabi'a.** (*oo-ree-doo nah-had bee shah-kel moo-kah-lah-mah mah-ah ah-sah-ah ah-sah-bee-ah;* I would like a wake-up call at 7:00.)

✔ **hal 'indakum mushrifat al-ghurfa?** (*hal een-dah-koom moosh-ree-fat al-ghoor-fah;* Do you have room service?)

Here are some phrases you might hear from the hotel staff:

✔ **ghurfatuka fii aT-Tabiq as-saadis.** (*ghoor-fah-too-kah fee ah-tah-beek ah-sah-dees.* Your room is located on the sixth floor.)

✔ **haa huwa al-miftaH.** (*hah hoo-wah al-meef-tah.* Here is your room key.)

✔ **hal 'indaka 'amti'a?** (*hal een-dah-kah am-tee-ah?* Do you have any luggage?)

✔ **al-Hammaal sa-yusaa'iduka 'ilaa al-ghurfa.** (*al-hah-mal sah-yoo-sah-ee-doo-kah ee-lah al-ghoor-fah.* The baggage handler will help you to your room.)

Checking Out of the Hotel

After your stay at the **funduq,** it's time for **waqt al-khuruuj** (*wah-ket al-koo-rooj;* checkout). The following phrases will help you check out on time:

✔ **mataa waqt al-khuruuj?** (*mah-tah wah-ket al-koo-rooj?* When is the checkout time?)

✔ **maa hiya al-faatuura al-'aama?** (*mah hee-yah al-fah-too-rah al-ah-mah?* What's the total bill?)

✔ **'uriidu 'iiSaala min faDlik.** (*oo-ree-doo ee-sah-lah meen fad-leek.* I'd like a receipt please.)

Before you leave the **funduq,** make sure you get all your stuff from your **ghurfa,** and take care of the bill. Some common extra charges to watch out for on your **faatuura** (*fah-too-rah;* bill) include:

> ✔ **faatuura al-haatif** (*fah-too-rah al-hah-teef;* telephone bill)
>
> ✔ **faatuura at-tilfaaz** (*fah-too-rah ah-teel-faz;* TV pay-per-view bill)
>
> ✔ **faatuura aT-Ta'aam** (*fah-too-rah ah-tah-am;* food bill)

When you pay the **faatuura,** it's a good idea to get an **'iiSaala** (*eeh-sah-lah;* receipt) in case you have a problem with the bill later on or can be reimbursed for your travel costs.

Life at Home

If you're like most people, you spend a lot of time at your **manzil** (*man-zeel;* house). The **manzil** is a bit different than the **bayt** (*bah-yet;* home) because a **manzil** can be any old **manzil,** whereas the **bayt** is the space where you feel most comfortable. In many cultures, a **manzil** is a family's or individual's most prized possession or asset.

As you know, a **manzil** consists of **ghuraf** (*ghoo-raf;* rooms). This list should help you become familiar with the major types of **ghuraf** in a **manzil:**

> ✔ **ghurfat al-juluus** (*ghoor-fat al-joo-loos;* sitting room)
>
> ✔ **ghurfat al-ma'iisha** (*ghoor-fat al-mah-ee-shah;* living room)
>
> ✔ **ghurfat al-'akl** (*ghoor-fat al-ah-kel;* dining room)
>
> ✔ **ghurfat an-nawm** (*ghoor-fat ah-nah-wem;* bedroom)
>
> ✔ **Hammaam** (*hah-mam;* bathroom)
>
> ✔ **ghurfat al-ghasl** (*ghoor-fat al-ghah-sel;* washing/laundry room)
>
> ✔ **maTbakh** (*mat-bak;* kitchen)

In addition to **ghuraf**, a **manzil** may also have a **karaaj** (*kah-raj;* garage) where you can park your **sayyaara** (*sah-yah-rah;* car), as well as a **bustaan** (*boos-tan;* garden) where you can play or just relax. Some **manaazil** (*mah-nah-zeel;* houses) even have a **masbaH** (*mas-bah;* swimming pool).

Each **ghurfa** in the **manzil** contains different items. For example, you can expect to find a **sariir** (*sah-reer;* bed) in a **ghurfat an-nawm.** Here are some items you can expect to find in the **Hammaam:**

- **mirHaaD** (*meer-had;* toilet)
- **duush** (*doosh;* shower)
- **maghsala** (*mag-sah-lah;* sink)
- **shawkat al-'asnaan** (*shaw-kat al-ass-nan;* toothbrush)
- **ghasuul as-sha'r** (*ghah-sool ah-shah-er;* shampoo)
- **Saabuun** (*sah-boon;* soap)
- **mir'aat** (*meer-at;* mirror)

You can expect to find the following items in the **maTbakh:**

- **furn** (*foo-ren;* stove)
- **tannuur** (*tah-noor;* oven)
- **thallaaja** (*thah-lah-jah;* refrigerator)
- **zubaala** (*zoo-bah-lah;* trash can)
- **shawkaat** (*shaw-kat;* forks)
- **malaa'iq** (*mah-lah-eek;* spoons)
- **sakaakiin** (*sah-kah-keen;* knives)
- **ku'uus** (*koo-oos;* glasses)
- **'aTbaaq** (*at-bak;* dishes)

Chapter 11

Dealing with Emergencies

• •

In This Chapter

▶ Finding help when you need it

▶ Talking with a doctor

▶ Getting legal help

• •

*H*andling an emergency in your native tongue can be difficult enough to deal with, and dealing with a situation in a foreign language such as Arabic may seem daunting. But don't panic! In this chapter, I give you the right words, phrases, and procedures to help you overcome an emergency situation — whether medical, legal, or political.

Shouting Out for Help

When you're witnessing or experiencing an emergency such as a theft, a fire, or even someone having a heart attack, your first instinct is to yell **musaa'ada** (*moo-sah-ah-dah;* help)! This section tells you which words to use to express your sense of emergency verbally in order to get the right kind of **musaa'ada**.

Arabic has two words that mean "help": **musaa'ada** (*moo-sah-ah-dah*) and **mu'aawana** (*moo-ah-wah-nah*). Both words are used interchangeably to ask for help in an emergency. You attract even more attention when you shout the words consecutively:

- ✔ **musaa'ada musaa'ada!** (*moo-sah-ah-dah moo-sah-ah-dah;* Help help!)

- ✔ **mu'aawana mu'aawana!** (*moo-ah-wah-nah moo-ah-wah-nah;* Help help!)

Arabic actually has a third word that means "help": **najda** (*nah-jeh-dah*). You can use **najda** to call for help, but be aware that screaming **najda** means that someone is in a severe, extremely dangerous, life-and-death situation. (If there were degrees to words for "help" — where level 3 is high and level 5 is extreme — **musaa'ada** and **mu'aawana** would be level 3s and **najda** would be a level 5.)

If you're witnessing or experiencing a drowning, a heart attack, or a suicide attempt, you should scream **najda** like this:

> **an-najda an-najda!** (*ahn-nah-jeh-dah ahn-nah-jeh-dah;* Help help!)

Here are some other important words and phrases to help you cope with an emergency:

- ✔ **saa'iduunii!** (*sah-ee-doo-nee;* Help me!)

- ✔ **'aawinuunii!** (*ah-wee-noo-nee;* Help me!)

- ✔ **shurTa!** (*shoo-reh-tah;* Police!)

- ✔ **'uriidu Tabiib!** (*oo-ree-doo tah-beeb;* I need a doctor!)

- ✔ **liSS!** (*lehs;* Thief!)

- ✔ **naar!** (*nahr;* Fire!)

A little help with the verb "to help"

The word **musaa'ada** is derived from the verb **saa'ada** (*sah-ah-dah*), which means "to help." Although screaming **musaa'ada** is an important first step to attract attention to an emergency, you also need to be able to coherently formulate a sentence in order to

get the right kind of help. Use the form
saa'ada to conjugate the verb "to help" in the
past tense and **yusaa'idu** (*yoo-sah-ee-doo*) to
conjugate it in the present tense. Table 11-1
shows the past tense. (Check out Chapter 2
for a quick reminder of the tenses.)

Table 11-1	The Past Tense of the Verb *saa'ada* (To Help)	
Form	*Pronunciation*	*Meaning*
'anaa saa'adtu	*ah-nah sah-ahd-too*	I helped
'anta saa'adta	*ahn-tah sah-ahd-tah*	You helped (MS)
'anti saa'adti	*ahn-tee sah-ahd-tee*	You helped (FS)
huwa saa'ada	*hoo-wah sah-ah-dah*	He helped
hiya saa'adat	*hee-yah sah-ah-daht*	She helped
naHnu saa'adnaa	*nah-noo sah-ahd-naa*	We helped
'antum saa'adtum	*ahn-toom sah-ahd-toom*	You helped (MP)
'antunna saa'adtunna	*ahn-too-nah sah-ahd-too-nah*	You helped (FP)
hum saa'aduu	*hoom sah-ah-doo*	They helped (MP)
hunna saa'adna	*hoo-nah sah-ahd-nah*	They helped (FP)
antumaa saa'adtumaa	*ahn-too-mah sah-ahd-too-mah*	You helped (dual/ MP/FP)
humaa saa'adaa	*hoo-mah sah-ah-dah*	They helped (dual/MP)
humaa saa'adataa	*hoo-mah sah-ah-dah-tah*	They helped (dual/FP)

Use the form **yusaa'idu** to conjugate "to help" in the present tense (see Table 11-2). Recall that the present tense in Arabic describes both a habitual action, such as "I help," and an ongoing action, such as "I am helping."

Table 11-2	The Present Tense of the Verb *yusaa'idu* (To Help)	
Form	*Pronunciation*	*Meaning*
'anaa 'usaa'idu	*ah-nah oo-sah-ee-doo*	I am helping
'anta tusaa'idu	*ahn-tah too-sah-ee-doo*	You are helping (MS)
'anti tusaa'idiina	*ahn-tee too-sah-ee-dee-nah*	You are helping (FS)
huwa yusaa'idu	*hoo-wah yoo-sah-ee-doo*	He is helping
hiya tusaa'idu	*hee-yah too-sah-ee-doo*	She is helping
naHnu nusaa'idu	*nah-noo noo-sah-ee-doo*	We are helping
'antum tusaa'iduuna	*ahn-toom too-sah-ee-doo-nah*	You are helping (MP)
'antunna tusaa'idna	*ahn-too-nah too-sah-eed-nah*	You are helping (FP)
hum yusaa'iduuna	*hoom yoo-sah-ee-doo-nah*	They are helping (MP)
hunna yusaa'idna	*hoo-nah yoo-sah-eed-nah*	They are helping (FP)
antumaa tusaa'idaani	*ahn-too-mah too-sah-ee-dah-nee*	You are helping (dual/MP/FP)
humaa yusaa'idaani	*hoo-mah yoo-sah-ee-dah-nee*	They are helping (dual/MP)
humaa tusaa'idaani	*hoo-mah too-sah-ee-dah-nee*	They are helping (dual/FP)

Although Arabic has more than one word for "help," **musaa'ada** is the most conjugated verb form. **mu'aawana** may also be conjugated using the form **'aawana** in the past tense and **yu'aawinu** in the present tense, but it's more of an archaic and arcane verb that isn't widely used in everyday Arabic. Because **najda** is more of a code word for distress, it doesn't have a verb equivalent form.

Lending a hand

Being in an emergency doesn't always mean that you're the one who needs help. You may be faced with a situation where you're actually the person who's in a position to offer help. The first thing you do in such a situation is ask questions to assess the damage and determine what course of action to take:

- ✔ **maadhaa waqa'a?** (*mah-zah wah-qah-ah;* What happened?)

- ✔ **hal kul shay' bikhayr?** (*hal kool shah-yeh bee-kayr;* Is everything all right?)

- ✔ **hal turiidu musaa'ada?** (*hal too-ree-doo moo-sah-ah-dah;* Do you want help?)

- ✔ **hal yajibu 'an tadhhab 'ilaa al-mustashfaa?** (*hal yah-jee-boo ann taz-hab ee-laa al-moos-tash-fah;* Do you need to go to the hospital?)

- ✔ **hal turiidu Tabiib?** (*hal too-ree-doo tah-beeb;* Do you want a doctor?)

If you're in a situation in which injuries are serious and the person appears to be disoriented, then you must take further steps, such as contacting the **shurTa** (*shoo-reh-tah;* police) or other first responders.

If you're ever in a situation where you need to call the police, you may say the following on the phone: **'aHtaaju bi musaa'ada fawran** (*ah-tah-joo bee moo-sah-ah-dah faw-ran;* I need help right away).

Here's an example of how you can ask someone whether they need help:

Lamia: **'afwan. hal kul shay' bikhayr?** (*ah-feh-wan. hal kool shah-yeh bee-kayr?* Excuse me. Is everything all right?)

Woman: **na'am. kul shay' bikhayr.** (*nah-am. kool shah-yeh bee-kayr.* Yes. Everything is all right.)

Lamia: **maadhaa waqa'a?** (*mah-zah wah-qah-ah?* What happened?)

Woman: **laa shay'. laqad saqaTtu.** (*lah shah-yeh. lah-kad sah-qah-too.* Nothing. I fell.)

Lamia: **hal turiidiina musaa'ada?** (*hal too-ree-dee-nah moo-sah-ah-dah?* Do you need help?)

Woman: **laa shukran. kul shay' sayakun bikhayr.** (*lah shook-ran. kool shah-yeh sah-yah-koon bee-kayr.* No thank you. I will be all right.)

Getting Medical Help

Visiting the doctor is sometimes essential, and this section introduces you to important medical terms to help you interact effectively with medical staff.

Locating the appropriate doctor

In case of a medical urgency, your first stop should be the **mustashfaa** (*moos-tash-fah;* hospital) to see a **Tabiib** (*tah-beeb;* doctor). If you simply need a checkup, go see a **Tabiib 'aam** (*tah-beeb ahm;* general doctor). If your needs are more specific, look for one of these specialist doctors:

- ✔ **Tabiib 'asnaan** (*tah-beeb ahs-nan;* dentist)
- ✔ **Tabiib 'aynayn** (*tah-beeb ah-yeh-nayn;* ophthalmologist)
- ✔ **Tabiib rijl** (*tah-beeb ree-jel;* orthopedist)
- ✔ **Tabiib 'aTfaal** (*tah-beeb aht-fal;* pediatrician)

Talking about your body

Locating the right doctor is only the first step toward getting treatment. In order to interact with the **Tabiib**, you need to be able to identify your different body parts in Arabic, explaining which parts hurt and which are fine. Table 11-3 lists all your major body parts.

Table 11-3	Body Parts	
Arabic	*Pronunciation*	*Translation*
jasad	*jah-sad*	body
ra's	*rahs*	head
fam	*fahm*	mouth
lisaan	*lee-sahn*	tongue
'asnaan	*ass-nahn*	teeth
wajh	*wah-jeh*	face
jild	*jee-led*	skin
'anf	*ah-nef*	nose
'udhunayn	*oo-zoo-nayn*	ears
'aynayn	*ah-yeh-nayn*	eyes
dimaagh	*dee-mag*	brain
qalb	*qah-leb*	heart
ri'a	*ree-ah*	lung
katef	*kah-tef*	shoulder
Sadr	*sah-der*	chest
ma'iida	*mah-ee-dah*	stomach
diraa'	*dee-rah*	arm
yad	*yahd*	hand
'aSaabi'	*ah-sah-beh*	fingers
rijl	*ree-jel*	leg
qadam	*qah-dam*	foot

(continued)

Table 11-3 *(continued)*

Arabic	Pronunciation	Translation
'aSaabi' al-qadam	*ah-sah-beh al-qah-dam*	toes
rukba	*roo-keh-bah*	knee
'aDHm	*ah-zem*	bone
damm	*deh-m*	blood
Dhahr	*zah-her*	back

Explaining your symptoms

The **Tabiib** can't provide you with the proper treatment unless you communicate the kind of pain you're experiencing. How **mariiD** (*mah-reed;* sick) do you feel? Do you have a **SuDaa'** (*soo-dah;* headache)? Or perhaps a **Haraara** (*hah-rah-rah;* fever)? Table 11-4 lists common symptoms.

Table 11-4   Common Symptoms

Arabic	Pronunciation	Translation
maraD	*mah-rad*	sickness
waja'	*wah-jah*	ache/ailment
su'aal	*soo-ahl*	cough
bard	*bah-red*	cold
Harq	*hah-rek*	burn
raDDa	*rah-dah*	bruise
waja' 'aDHhar	*wah-jah ah-zah-her*	backache
maraD al-Hasaasiya	*mah-rad al-hah-sah-see-yah*	allergy

When you go to the **Tabiib,** he or she may ask you, **maadha yu'limuka?** (*mah-zah yoo-lee-moo-kah;* What hurts you?). The most common way to respond to this question is to name the body part that hurts followed by **yu'limunii** (*yoo-lee-moo-nee;* hurts me).

So when the **Tabiib** asks **maadha yu'limuka?**, you may say:

> ✔ **ra'sii yu'limunii.** (*rah-see yoo-lee-moo-nee;* My head hurts me.)

> ✔ **Sadrii yu'limunii.** (*sah-der-ee yoo-lee-moo-nee.* My chest hurts me.)

> ✔ **diraa'ii yu'limunii.** (*dee-rah-ee yoo-lee-moo-nee.* My arm hurts me.)

Getting treatment

After the **Tabiib** analyzes your symptoms, he or she is able to offer you **'ilaaj** (*ee-laj;* treatment). Following the **Tabiib**'s orders is important for both getting and remaining **saliim** (*sah-leem;* healthy), so pay attention. Here are treatment-related words you may encounter:

> ✔ **dawaa'** (*dah-wah;* medicine)

> ✔ **SayDaliiyya** (*sah-yeh-dah-lee-yah;* pharmacy)

> ✔ **'iyaada** (*ee-yah-dah;* clinic)

The following is a sample conversation between a doctor and a patient:

Doctor: **maadha yu'limuka?** (*mah-zah yoo-lee-moo-kah?* What hurts you?)

Omar: **ra'sii yu'limunii.** (*rah-see yoo-lee-moo-nee.* My head hurts.)

Doctor: **shay' 'aakhar?** (*shah-y ah-kar?* Anything else?)

Omar: **na'am. 'indii Haraara.** (*nah-am. een-dee hah-rah-rah.* Yes. I have a fever.)

Doctor: **khudh haadhaa 'asbiriin wa satakuun bikhayr.** (*kooz hah-zah ass-pee-reen wah sah-tah-koon bee-kah-yer.* Take this aspirin, and you will be all right.)

Words to Know

mariiD	mah-reed	sick
'ilaaj	ee-laj	treatment
saliim	sah-leem	healthy
sharaab su'aal	shah-rahb soo-all	cough medicine
Suurat 'ashi'a	soo-rat ah-shee-ah	X-ray
'asbiriin	ass-pee-reen	aspirin

Acquiring Legal Help

Let's hope it's never the case, but you may have a run-in with the law and need the services of a **muHaamiiy** (*moo-hah-mee;* lawyer). The **muHaamiiy** has a good understanding of the **qaanuun** (*qah-noon;* law) and is in a position to help you if you're ever charged with committing a **mujrima** (*mooj-ree-mah;* crime).

If you happen to be in a foreign country and need legal representation, the best route is to contact your country's **qunSuliyya** (*koon-soo-lee-yah;* consulate) and ask to speak to

the **qunSul** (*koon-sool;* consul). Because consular officers have a very good understanding of the laws of their host countries, you
may be better off getting help directly from
them rather than finding your own
muHaamiiy. Especially if it looks like you
have to go to **maHkama** (*mah-kah-mah;*
court) and face a qaadiiy (*qah-dee;* judge),
the help a **qunSuliyya** can provide is
invaluable.

You may also want to call your country's **sifaara**
(*see-fah-rah;* embassy) if you're in a really serious situation. Even if you're unable to talk to the **safiir** (*sah-
feer;* ambassador) directly, your **sifaara** may take the
appropriate steps to provide you with assistance.

Chapter 12

Ten Favorite Arabic Expressions

- -

A rabic uses a lot of colorful expressions and words. Here are ten of the best.

marHaba bikum!

mahr-hah-bah bee-koom; Welcome to all of you!

This term of welcoming is extremely popular with Arabic speakers. It's usually said with a lot of zest and enthusiasm and is often accompanied by very animated hand gestures. It's not uncommon for someone to say **marHaba bikum** and then proceed to hug you or give you a kiss on the cheek. This expression is a very affectionate form of greeting someone, such as an old friend, a very special guest, or a close relative. But the relationship doesn't necessarily have to be a close one — if you're ever invited into a Middle Eastern home for a dinner or a lunch, don't be surprised if the host jovially shouts **marHaba bikum** and gives you a great big bear hug!

mumtaaz!

moom-tahz; Excellent!

This expression is a way to note that something is going very well. A teacher may tell her students **mumtaaz** if they conjugate a difficult Arabic verb in the past tense, or a fan may yell **mumtaaz** if his team scores a goal against an opponent. **mumtaaz** is used during joyous events or as a sign of encouragement. It's a very positive word that Arabic speakers like to use because it connotes a positive attitude.

al-Hamdu li-llah

al-hahm-doo lee-lah; Praise to God

al-Hamdu li-llah is a part of everyday Arabic. Arabic speakers say **al-Hamdu li-llah** after performing almost any task, including finishing a meal, drinking water, finishing a project at work, and running an errand. The expression's extensive application goes beyond completing tasks; for example, if someone asks you **kayf al-Haal?** (*kah-yef al-hal;* How are you doing?), you may reply **al-Hamdu li-llah** and mean "Praise to God; I'm doing well." Because of its versatility, it's customary to hear **al-Hamdu li-llah** quite often when native speakers are talking to each other.

inshaa' allah

een-shah-ah ah-lah; If God wishes it

If you've ever watched Arabic speakers on Arabic TV, you've probably heard them use the expression **inshaa' allah.** This expression, which literally means "If God wishes it" or "If God wills it," is very popular among Arabic speakers when discussing future events. It's almost a rule that whenever someone brings up an event that will take place in the future, the expression **inshaa' allah** follows soon after. For example, when someone asks you how you think you're going to do on your next exam, you say, **'ata-mannaa 'an 'anjaH inshaa' allah** (*ah-tah-mah-nah ann an-jaheen-shah-ah ah-lah;* I hope I do well, if God wishes it).

mabruk!

mahb-rook; Blessing upon you!

The root of the word **mabruk** is the noun **baraka** (*bah-rah-kah*), which means "blessing." **mabruk** is used at joyous occasions, such as the birth of a baby or a wedding ceremony. Though its strict interpretation is "Blessing upon you," **mabruk** is just like saying "Congratulations." When you say **mabruk,** make sure you say it with a lot of energy and enthusiasm!

bi 'idni allah

bee eed-nee ah-lah; With God's guidance

This expression is meant to motivate and offer support and guidance, and although this expression contains a reference to God, it's actually a lot less common than expressions such as **inshaa' allah** or **al-Hamdu li-llah.** That's because **bii 'idni allah** is used only during very special occasions, when one is facing serious challenges or is having difficulty in life, marriage, work, or school. Whenever someone's facing hardship, it's common for him or her to say **sa-'uwaajihu haadhihi as-su'uubu bi 'idni allah** (*sah-oo-wah-jee-hoo hah-zee-hee ah-so-oo-boo bee eed-nee ah-lah;* I will face this difficulty, with God's guidance).

bi SaHHa

bee sah-hah; With strength

Even though this expression literally means "with strength," it's not necessarily used in a context of encouragement or support like **bi 'idni allah** is. Rather, **bi SaHHa** is an appropriate thing to say after someone has finished a difficult task and can relax.

For example, if a friend has wrapped up writing a book, closed a big deal, or ended a difficult case, you may say to him **bi SaHHa,** which signifies that your friend will be stronger as a result of accomplishing what he's accomplished and now can rest a bit.

taHiyyaat

tah-hee-yat; Regards

taHiyyaat is a religious term that Muslims use when they're praying. After a Muslim finishes praying, he performs the **taHiyyaat** by turning once to the right and once to the left, acknowledging the two angels that Muslims believe guard each person. In addition to its religious affiliation, Arabic speakers commonly use **taHiyyaat** to send their regards. For instance, a friend may say to you, **salaam 'an 'abuuka** (*sah-lam ann ah-boo-kah;* Say hello to your father for me.) Similarly, to send your regards to a friend, you say, **taHiyyaat.**

muballagh

moo-bah-lag; Equally

muballagh is an expression that's similar to **taHiyyaat** in that you use it to send regards. However, unlike **taHiyyaat, muballagh** is a response; that is, you use it *after* someone sends their regards to you. So if someone says to you, **salaam 'an 'ukhtuk** (*sah-lam ann ook-took;* Say hello to your sister for me), you respond, **muballagh.** Responding with this expression means that you acknowledge the message and thank the person for it on behalf of your sister. So make sure to say **muballagh** only after someone sends their regards — not before!

tabaaraka allah

tah-bah-rah-kah ah-lah; With God's blessing

This expression is the equivalent of "God bless you" in English; it's most commonly used among close friends or family members to congratulate each other on accomplishments, achievements, or other happy events. For instance, if a son or daughter receives a good grade on an exam, the parents would say, **tabaaraka allah.** Another very popular use for this expression is to express warmth and joy toward kids.

Chapter 13

Ten Great Arabic Proverbs

. . . .

*E*ven if you've read only a few chapters of this book, you've probably figured out that Arabic is a very poetic language. One aspect of the language that reinforces its poetic nature is the use of **'amthila** (*am-thee-lah;* proverbs). Proverbs play an important role in the Arabic language. If you're having a conversation with an Arabic speaker or listening to Arabic speakers converse among themselves, don't be surprised to hear proverbs peppered throughout the conversation. This chapter introduces you to some of the more common and flowery proverbs of the Arabic language.

al-'amthaal noor al-kalaam.

al-am-thal noor al-kah-lam; Proverbs are the light of speech.

The role of proverbs in Arabic is so important that there's a proverb on the importance of proverbs!

'a'mal khayr wa 'ilqahu fii al-baHr.

ah-mal kah-yer wah eel-qah-hoo fee al-bah-her; Do good and cast it into the sea.

Arab culture emphasizes humility and modesty.
This proverb means that when you commit a chari-
table act, you shouldn't go around boasting about it;
rather, you should "cast it into the sea" where no one
can find out about it.

'uTlubuu al-'ilm min al-mahd 'ilaa al-laHd.

oot-loo-boo al-ee-lem meen al-mahd ee-lah al-lah-hed;
Seek knowledge from the cradle to the grave.

al-'ilm (*al-ee-lem;* knowledge) is an important virtue
in Arabic culture. Arabs have produced some of the
greatest legal, medical, and scientific minds in history, in no small part because Arabs like to instill in
their children a lifelong desire to learn and continue
learning every single day of one's existence.

yad waaHida maa tusaffiq.

yad wah-hee-dah mah too-sah-feek; A hand by itself
cannot clap.

This proverb, which is common in the West but origi-
nates in Arab culture, underscores the importance of
teamwork, cooperation, and collaboration.

al-Harbaa' laa Yughaadir shajaratuh hattaa yakun mu'akkid 'an shajara 'ukhraa.

*al-har-bah lah yoo-gah-deer shah-jah-rah-tooh hah-tah
yah-koon moo-ah-keed ann shah-jah-rah ook-rah;* The

chameleon does not leave his tree until he is sure of another.

This proverb stresses the importance of foresight, planning, and looking ahead. A chameleon that is mindful of predators won't change trees until it knows that it'll be safe in the next tree it goes to.

khaTa' ma'roof 'aHsan min Haqiiqa ghayr ma'roofa.

kah-tah mah-roof ah-san meen hah-kee-kah gah-yer mah-roo-fah; A known mistake is better than an unknown truth.

This metaphysical proverb has a deep meaning: It's better for you to identify and learn from a mistake than not to know a truth at all. In the debate of known versus unknown knowledge, this proverb indicates that knowing is better than not knowing, even if what you know is not an absolute truth.

as-sirr mithel al-Hamaama: 'indamaa yughaadir yadii yaTiir.

ah-seer mee-thel al-hah-mah-mah: een-dah-mah yoo-gah-deer yah-dee yah-teer; A secret is like a dove: When it leaves my hand, it flies away.

A secret is meant to be kept close to your chest — in other words, you shouldn't divulge a secret. As soon as you let a secret out of your "hand," it flies away and spreads around. Just as a dove won't leave unless you release it, a secret won't become known unless you divulge it.

al-'aql li an-niDHaar wa al-kalb li as-simaa'.

al-ah-kel lee ah-nee-zar wah al-kah-leb lee ah-see-mah;
The mind is for seeing, and the heart is for hearing.

The mind is to be used for analytical purposes: observation and analysis. The heart, on the other hand, is for emotions; you should listen and feel with your heart.

kul yawm min Hayaatuk SafHa min taariikhuk.

kool yah-oum meen hah-yah-took saf-hah meen tah-ree-kook; Every day of your life is a page of your history.

You only live one life, so you should enjoy every single day. At the end, each day's experiences are what make up your history.

li faatik bi liila faatik bi Hiila.

lee fah-tek bee lee-lah fah-tek bee hee-lah; He who surpasses (is older than) you by one night surpasses you by one idea.

In Arabic culture and society, maturity and respect for elders is a highly regarded virtue. This proverb reinforces the idea that elders are respected, and their counsel is sought often.

Index

• A •

above, 25
accommodations
    hotels, 159–168
    house, 168–169
accounting department, 124
accounting firm, 123
ache/ailment, 178
additional, 129
adjectives
    common, 18–19, 95
    comparative forms, 96–98
    described, 17
    superlatives, 98–99
after, 46
afternoon, 46
agree, 94
airplane
    boarding the plane, 143
    immigration and customs,
        145–147
    registering at the airport,
        141–142
    reservations/ticket, 137–139
airport, 141–142
airport terminal, 142
aisle seat, 139
alcohol, customs restrictions,
    146
all sorts, 79
allergy, 178
alphabet
    about, 7
    consonants, 10–14
    diphthongs, 10
    vowels, 7–10
ambassador, 181
appetizers, 84
appointment, 133–134
April, 50

Arabic
    favorite expressions,
        183–187
    Koranic Arabic, 1–2
    Modern Standard Arabic
        (MSA), 2
    musical instruments,
        115–116
    origins of English words, 5–7
    regional dialects, 2
    scholars, 104
    transcription, 15–16
    writing and reading from
        right to left, 7
Arabic characters
    for consonants, 11–14
    learning, 16
    for long vowels, 10
are/is sentence, 27–28
around, 105
arrival, 143
to arrive, 144–145
art, 105
articles, definite and
        indefinite, 19–21
asking for directions
    asking with courtesy, 152
    Could you repeat that?,
        153–154
    using command forms,
        155–157
    "where" questions, 151–153
asking questions, 63–64
asking to speak to someone,
    133
aspirin, 180
ate, 33
ATM, 53, 54
attendant, 162
August, 51
available, 162

• B •

backache, 178
bad, 95
baggage handler/porter, 147
bakery, 89
bank
  account, 52–54
  ATM, 53, 54
  deposit, 53, 54
  exchanging currency, 55–56
bank teller, 53
banker, 123
bathing suit, 115
bathroom, 162, 168, 169
bathtub, 162
beach, 115
beach umbrella, 115
beautiful, 19, 94
beauty parlor, 90
bed, 169
bedroom, 168
beef, 76
beginning, 128
behind, 25, 152
below, 152
beverages, 85
bicycle, 148
big, 18, 95
bill, paying
  hotel, 167–168
  restaurant, 87
birthday, 146
blanket, 162
Blessing upon you! (favorite
      expression), 185
boarding the plane, 143
body parts, 177–178
book, 18, 20, 64, 131
bookstore/library, 89
boy(s), 18, 92
bread, 74
breakfast, 74–76
briefcase, 142, 166
bruise, 178
burn, 178
bus, 149–150, 155
bus driver, 150

bus schedule, 150
bus station/stop, 149
bus ticket, 149
business appointments,
      133–134
businessman, 123
busy, 134

• C •

calendars, 50–51
car, 18, 148, 169
cards, 117
cart, 147
cash, 52, 149
cellphone, 132
Celsius, converting to
      Fahrenheit, 71
chair, 131
change, money, 149
cheap, 95
check(s), 52
chess, 117
chicken, 77, 82
classified ads, 119
client(s), 123
clinic, 179
close, 155
close to, 25
clothes shopping, 100–102
clothing store, 89
cloud, 115
coffee, 74
coin(s), 52
cold, 70, 178
colleagues, 124–128
color, 94, 101–102
command forms/imperative
      verbs
  asking for directions,
      155–157
  giving orders, 129–130
company, 120, 123, 134
computer, 131
concierge, 166
condiments, 77
consonants, 10–14
consulate, 180–181

conversation
  asking questions, 63–64
  with colleagues, 124–128
  countries and nationalities,
      61–63
  greetings, 57–59
  introductions, 60–61
  telephone, 132–133
  weather, 69–71
  work, 67–69
  yourself and your family,
      65–67
copies, 129
cough, 178
cough medicine, 180
counter/meter (taxi), 148, 149
counting, 42–43
country, 55
country names, 62–63
credit card(s), 52, 53, 54
currency, 52, 55
currency exchange, 55–56
customers, 100
customs and immigration,
    145–147

• *D* •

dancing, 117
date of birth, 146
day after tomorrow, 46
day before yesterday, 46
days of the week, 49–50
debit card, 52, 53, 54
December, 51
definite and indefinite articles,
    19–21
definite clause, 27
definite phrases, 22
demonstratives
  common, 92–94
  comparative sentences with,
      97–98
  using, 26–28
dentist, 176
department store/mall, 90
departure, 143
deposit, 53, 54

desk clerk, 131, 165, 166
desserts, 84–85
dialects, regional, 2
dialing a phone, 132
dictionary, 38–39
did, 33
difference, 53
different, 100
dining. See meals; restaurant
dining room, 82, 168
dining table, 82–83
dinner, 81–82
diphthongs, 10
directions
  asking for, 91, 151–157
  inside, 92
  left, 92
  outside, 92
  right, 92
discounts, hotel, 163
distribute, 128
doctor
  explaining symptoms to,
      178–179
  locating, 176
  talking about your body,
      177–178
  treatment, 179–180
dominant vowel, 38
drawing/carving, 105, 116
drinks, 85
drums, 116
dual, 29

• *E* •

east, 157
to eat, 80–81
eat, 130
Egyptian dialect, 2
elders, respect for, 192
electronics store, 89
elevator, 92, 166
embassy, 181
emergencies
  doctor, 176–180
  hospital, 176
  legal, 180–181

emergencies *(continued)*
  offering help, 175–176
  shouting for help, 171–175
  symptoms, 178–179
employees, 120
employer, 120
ending, 128
English words, Arabic origins
    of, 5–7
entertaining, 105
entertainment, 105
entrance, 105
entrees, 84
entry, 147
Equally (favorite expression),
    186
eraser, 131
etiquette
  for asking a question, 153
  for visiting a mosque,
    109–110
evening, 46
every, 150
Excellent! (favorite
    expression), 183–184
exchange desk, 55–56
exchanging currency, 55–56
excuse me/pardon me, 153
exit, 105, 146
expensive, 95
expressions, Arabic favorite,
    183–187

• *F* •

factory, 123
Fahrenheit, 71
fall, 71
family, 65–67, 115
far, 95, 155
far from, 25
fare, 149
fast, 95
father, 65
favorite expressions, Arabic,
    183–187
fax machine, 131
February, 50

fees, 53, 54
fever, 178
firefighter, 123
fish, 77, 82
fish store, 90
flight, 139
flight attendant, 143
floor, 92, 166
flute, 116
follow, 94
food, 73
food bill, hotel, 168
Friday, 50
friends, 115, 119, 125
from, 25
fruit, list of, 76
furniture and supplies,
    131–132
future tense verbs, 39–40

• *G* •

garage, 169
garden, 169
gate, 142
girl(s), 18, 92
giving orders, 129–130
glue, 131
to go, 107–108
go, 155
goal/purpose, 146
God bless you (favorite
    expression), 187
good, 95
good evening, 61
Good luck!, 57
good night, 61
goodbye, 58–59
greetings. See also small talk
  about, 57
  with colleagues, 124–125
  goodbye, 58–59
  hello, 58, 132
  How are you doing?, 59
  I am from…, 62–63
  I'm doing well, 59, 61
  My name is…., 60
  phone message, 135
  What's your name?, 60

Gregorian calendar, 50–51
grocery store, 89
guitar, 116
Gulf Arabic dialect, 2

• *H* •

hairdresser, 90
the Hajj (pilgrimage), 110–111
half, 128
handsome, 19
he, 33
headache, 178
health insurance, 120
health symptoms, 178–179
healthy, 179
heavy, 95
he/it, 29
hello, 58, 132
to help, 172–175
help
  offering, 175–176
  shouting for, 171–175
help you, 134
here, 155
Hijaab (veil), 146
hobbies, 116–117
holiday season, 164
holiday/vacation, 120, 139,
    159
home, 168
home-cooked meals, 82–83
hospital, 176
host, 121
hot, 70
hotel
  about, 159–160
  checking in, 165–167
  checking out, 167–168
  choosing, 160–162
  length of stay, 164–165
  phone bill, 168
  price, 163
  reservations, 162–165
hour, 46
house, 168–169
how, 63

how many, 63
how much, 63
human resources department,
    124
humidity, 70
hungry, 73
husband, 65

• *I* •

I believe, 157
I don't understand, 153
icons used in this book, 3
ID card, 150
If God wishes it (favorite
    expression), 184
I/me, 29
immigrant(s), 147
immigration and customs,
    145–147
imperative verbs/command
    forms
  asking for directions,
    155–157
  giving orders, 129–130
in, 25
in front of, 25, 152
included, 166
indefinite and definite articles,
    19–21
indefinite phrases, 21–22
information, 122, 165
inside, 92
instructions, 143
interest rate, 53
interests, 119
interview, 120–121
introductions
  It's a pleasure to meet
    you, 60
  My name is, 60
  nice to meet you, 60, 61
  What's your name?, 60
is/are sentence, 27–28
Islamic calendar, 50, 51–52

• J •

January, 50
jellaba (traditional
        garment), 83
jeweler, 90
job/work. See also office
        environment
    finding, 119–122
    professions, list of, 68, 123
    schedule for workdays,
        122–123
    talking about, 67–69
    telephone, 132–136
July, 51
June, 51

• K •

keep, 149
keys, hotel, 166
kitchen, 82, 168, 169
knitting, 117
knowledge, 190
Koranic Arabic, 1–2

• L •

lamb, 76
lamp, 162
laundry room, 168
law firm, 123
lawyer, 123, 180
left, 92
left of, 152
legal, 180–181
leisure
    beach, 115
    hobbies, 116–117
    movies, 106–109
    museums, 103–105
    musical instruments,
        115–116
    religious sites, 109–111
    sports, 111–115
length of stay, hotel, 164–165
let's go, 114–115
library, 89

light, 20
light (weight), 95
living room, 168
look, 130
luggage, 142, 166
lunch, 76–80, 122

• M •

machines, 131
madam, 125
marble, 105
March, 50
marketing department, 124
May, 51
meals. See also restaurant
    about, 73
    breakfast, 74–76
    dinner, 81–82
    to eat, 80–81
    home-cooked, 82–83
    lunch, 76–80
meat, 76, 82
Mecca, Saudi Arabia, 110
medical emergencies, 176–180
medicine, 179
meeting/conference, 128, 134
men, 92
menu, 83–85
message, 135
meter, taxi, 148, 149
Middle Eastern music, 116
milk, 74
minutes, 46, 47–48
mirror, 162
Modern Standard Arabic
        (MSA), 2
Monday, 50
money
    about, 52
    ATM, 53, 54
    bank account, 52–54
    currency exchange, 55–56
months, 50–51, 122
moon letters, 20
morning, 46
mosque, visiting, 109–110
mother, 65

motorcycle, 148
move, 130
movies, 106–109
Mr./Sir, 134
MSA (Modern Standard
    Arabic), 2
museums, 103–105
music, 115–116
musical instruments, 115–116
my name, 60, 61

• **N** •

name, 61, 135
name of countries, 62–63
nationality, 62–63, 146
near, 95
new, 95
newspaper, 119
next to, 25
night, 46
noon, 46
north, 157
North African dialect, 2
notebook, 131
nouns
    common, 18
    described, 17–18
    possessive, 161
November, 51
number, phone, 132, 135
numbers
    about, 41
    counting, 42–43
    ordinals, 43–45

• **O** •

ocean, 115
October, 51
of course, 156
"of" or "to," 48–49
offering, 122
office environment. See also
        job/work
    about, 122
    departments, 123–124
    furniture and supplies,
        131–132

giving orders, 129–130
interacting with colleagues,
    124–128
key words and terms,
    123, 128–129
phone conversations,
    132–136
schedule for workdays, 122
writing reports, 126–128
okay, 157
old, 95
on, 25
only, 79
to open, 105
ophthalmologist, 176
order, 79
ordering at restaurant, 85–87
orders, giving, 129–130
ordinal numbers, 43–45
orthopedist, 176
outside, 92

• **P** •

pain symptoms, 178–179
painting, 105
paper clip, 131
papers, 131
pardon me/excuse me, 153
parents, 65
particular, 94, 100
passenger, 143
passport, 142
past tense verbs, 33–36
pastry shop, 89
pay-per-view, 168
pediatrician, 176
pencil, 131
pension, 120, 131
percentage, 53
personal pronouns
    forming "to be" sentences,
        28–30
    prefixes and suffixes, 37–38
    suffixes for verbs in the past
        tense, 34–35
    to use with imperatives,
        129–130
pharmacy, 179

phone
about, 132
asking to speak to someone, 133
beginning a conversation, 132–133
cellphone, 132
dialing, 132
greeting message, 135
hotel phone bill, 168
making business appointments, 133–134
voice mail, 135–136
phone card, 132
phone number, 132, 135
photocopier, 131
piano, 116
pictures, 128
pilgrimage to Mecca (the Hajj), 110–111
pillow, 162
plane
boarding, 143
immigration and customs, 145–147
registering at the airport, 141–142
reservations/ticket, 137–139
plane ticket, 137–139
to play, 112–114, 116, 117
poetry, 117
police, 123, 175
porter/baggage handler, 147
position, 122
possessive noun, 161
pottery, 116
Praise to God (favorite expression), 184
prefixes, 37–38
prepositions
after comparative adjectives, 96
building sentences with, 25–26
list of most common, 152
"of" or "to," 48–49
present tense verbs, 36–39

president, 134
pretty/beautiful, 95, 105
price, 163
printer, 131
professional, 123
professions, list of, 68, 123. See also work/job
pronouns, personal
forming "to be" sentences, 28–30
prefixes and suffixes, 37–38
suffixes for verbs in the past tense, 34–35
to use with imperatives, 129–130
pronunciation of difficult letters, 15
proverbs, 189–192
public phone, 132
purpose/goal, 146

• Q •

questions
answering at airport, 142
asking for directions, 151–157
asking with courtesy, 152
Could you repeat that?, 153–154
immigration and customs, 145–146
key question words, 63–64

• R •

radio, 162
rain, 69
rainbow, 70
reading, 116
reading from right to left, 7
ready, 128, 130
receipt, hotel, 168
reception/reception desk, 166
Regards (favorite expression), 186
regional dialects, 2

registering at the airport,
    141–142
registration desk, 142
religious prayer, 109–110
religious sites
    the Hajj (pilgrimage),
        110–111
    visiting a mosque, 109–110
rental car, 148
repeat, 130, 155
reports, writing, 126–128
representative(s), 129
reservations
    airplane, 137–138
    hotel, 162–165
restaurant. See also meals
    about, 83
    menu, 83–85
    paying the bill, 87
    placing an order, 85–87
    tipping the waiter/
        waitress, 87
rice, 77
right, 92
right of, 152
room, 128, 160–161, 168
room staff, 162
rules, 109

• *S* •

safe deposit box, 162
salad, 77
salary, 120
sand, 115
sandwich, 77–79
Saturday, 50
saw, 33, 105
saxophone, 116
say, 130
schedule for workdays, 122
school, 20
script. See Arabic characters
searching, 91
seasons, 71
seat, 121, 139, 143
secretary/assistant, 134
section, 91

selection, 100
sentence, 24
sentences
    to be, 23, 28–33
    is/are, 23–24
    using demonstratives, 27–28
    using prepositions, 25–26
    was/were, 32–33
    without verbs, 23–24
September, 51
she/it, 29
ship, 148
shoes, 109
shopping
    asking for an item, 92–94
    browsing, 90–91
    clothes, 100–102
    comparing merchandise,
        95–98
    department stores, 90
    getting around stores, 91–92
    grocery stores, 89
    newspaper, 119
    picking the best item,
        98–100
    specialty stores, 89–90
short, 19
shouting for help, 171–175
shower, 162
sick, 180
sink, 162
sir, 125, 134
sister, 125
sitting room, 168
size, 79
skills, 119
slow, 95
small, 19, 95
small talk
    asking questions, 63–64
    countries and nationalities,
        61–63
    greetings, 57–59
    introductions, 60–61
    weather, 69–71
    work, 67–69
    yourself and your family,
        65–67

snack, 73
snow, 70
soccer, 111, 114–115
south, 157
speak, 130
speak slowly please, 153
speaking Arabic, 15
sports, 111–115
spring, 71
stapler, 131
station, 155
to stay, 165
stop, 130, 156
store clerk, 90
stores
  browsing, 90–91
  getting around, 91–92
  types of, 89–90
storm, 70
student, 18, 163
subway, 148
suffixes
  personal pronoun suffixes,
    34–35
  for verbs in the present
    tense, 37–38
suitcase, 142, 166
summer, 71
sun, 69, 115
sun letters, 20–21
Sunday, 50
sunrise, 46
sunscreen, 115
sunset, 46
superlatives, 98–99
supplies for office, 131–132
sweets, 85
swimming pool, 169

● *T* ●

table, 18, 82–83
take, 155
tall, 19
tape, 131
taxi, 148–149, 155
taxi driver, 148
tea, 74

teacher, 18
telephone
  about, 132
  asking to speak to someone,
    133
  beginning a conversation,
    132–133
  cellphone, 132
  dialing, 132
  greeting message, 135
  hotel phone bill, 168
  making business
    appointments, 133–134
  phone card, 132
  voice mail, 135–136
temperature, 69, 70, 71
thank you, 59
that, 26, 93
then, 157
there, 155
these/those, 27, 93
they, 29
this, 26, 93
Thursday, 50
ticket, 139, 149
time
  of day, 46–47
  days and months, 49–52
  minutes, 46, 47–49
  telling, 45–46
time of the call, 135
tipping
  taxi, 149
  waiter/waitress, 87
to, 25
to add, 128
"to be" sentences
  described, 23
  negative (not to be), 30–31
  past tense (was/were),
    32–33
  using personal pronouns,
    28–30
to offer, 122
to open, 53
"to" or "of," 48–49
to organize, 142
to print, 129

to register, 142
to try, 94
today, 46
tomorrow, 46
tour, 105
tourism, 147
tourist, 147
towel, 162
train, 150, 155
transcription used in this
    book, 15–16
transliteration, 2
transportation
    about, 137, 147–148
    airplane, 137–147
    asking for directions,
        151–157
    bus, 149–150, 155
    taxi, 148–149, 155
    train, 150, 155
to travel, 140–141
travel agency, 90
travel agent, 138
traveler(s), 140, 145
traveler's checks, 55
treatment, medical, 179–180
trip, 140, 159
trumpet, 116
Tuesday, 50
turn, 156
type/kind, 53, 79, 94

• *U* •

ugly, 95
underneath, 25
understand, 155
university, 119
until next time, 61

• *V* •

vacation/holiday, 120, 139, 159
veal, 76
vegetables, list of, 77
veil (Hijaab), 146

verbs
    future tense, 39–40
    imperative, 129–130,
        155–157
    past tense, 33–36
    present tense, 36–39
    sentences without, 23–24
very, 105
violin, 116
visa, 142
voice mail, 135–136
vowels
    dominant, 38–39
    double vowels, 8–9
    long vowels, 9–10
    main vowels, 7–8
voyage, 140

• *W* •

waiter/waitress, 85–87
walk, 156
was/were sentences, 32–33
water, 85
wave, 115
we, 29
weather
    rain, 69
    seasons, 71
    talking about, 69–71
    temperature, 69, 70, 71
Wednesday, 50
Welcome to all of you!
        (favorite expression), 183
west, 157
Western civilization, 104
what, 63
when, 63
"where" questions, 151–153
white bread, 79
who, 63
whole wheat bread, 79
why, 63
wife, 65
will open, 105
wind, 70

window seat, 140
winter, 71, 162
with, 25
With God's blessing. (favorite
    expression), 187
With God's guidance! (favorite
    expression), 185
With strength (favorite
    expression), 185–186
withdrawal, 54
women, 91
workers, 122
work/job. See also office
    environment
  finding, 119–122
  professions, list of, 68, 123
  schedule for workdays,
    122–123
  talking about, 67–69
  telephone, 132–136

would like, 134
to write
  future tense, 40
  imperative form, 130
  past tense, 33–34
  present tense, 36–37
writing Arabic, 7
writing reports, 126–128

• *X* •

X-ray, 180

• *Y* •

yesterday, 46
you, 29
your visit, 105
youth hostel, 163

FOR DUMMIES®

The easy way to get more done and have more fun